"Look Up and Live"

Taking Dominion Over Diagnosis!

by
Yvette Bell

Copyright © 2021 Yvette Bell Ministries

ALL RIGHTS RESERVED. This book contains material protected under International and Federal Copyright Laws and Treaties. Any unauthorized reprint or use of this material is prohibited. No part of this book may be reproduced or transmitted in any form or by any means, electronic or mechanical, including photocopying, recording, or by any information storage and retrieval system without express written permission from the author/publisher.

Unless otherwise noted all Scripture quotations are taken from the King James Version of the Bible. All rights reserved.

Scripture taken from the New King James Version®.
Copyright © 1982 by Thomas Nelson. Used by permission. All rights reserved.

Editing & Book Cover Design: Legacy Driven Consulting
www.legacydrivenconsulting.com.

Printed by: Prize Publishing House, LLC in the United States of America.

Second printing edition 2021.
Prize Publishing House
P.O. Box 9856 Chesapeake, VA 23321
www.PrizePublishingHouse.com

ISBN: 978-1-7364457-8-5

ISBN (E-Book): 978-1-7364457-9-2

"Declare ye among the nations, publish, and set up a standard; publish and conceal not". – Jeremiah 50:2

Table of Contents

Dedication vii

Acknowledgements viii

Foreword xii

Introduction xv

Chapter One

Taking Dominion After Diagnosis 18

Chapter Two

Voices of Influence 30

Chapter Three

Becoming Vulnerable & Transparent 40

Chapter Four

Transformative Trauma 47

Chapter Five

A Family's Journey 56

Chapter Six

Our Story, God's Glory 66

Chapter Seven

Look Up and Live 72

About the Author 95
Additional Resources by the Author 97
Endnotes 102

Dedication

I dedicate this book to all those who have been diagnosed with, or have lost loved ones to, any form of cancer or chronic disease. Each one of you are my personal heroes. Unless one faces the health challenges you have, they cannot truly understand the endurance it takes to overcome. I pray that the personal testimony written in this book, encourages each of you to continue to take courage and find a way to tell others your stories. For your story is unique, and you are the only expert of your own experiences that will encourage others to look up and live.

Most of all, to the love, mercy, grace, and miracle working power of Christ Jesus. With Him "All Things Are Possible" if we can just believe!

Acknowledgements

To my dearest husband and that covering, Daryl. You are truly my life partner and coach sent from God directly to me. This was your journey too. I pray the words of this book affirm you and help you in your continued healing as well. Thank you for helping me push through fears and doubts to get to my blessed place in Jesus Christ. To finally obey God has been such a lift of weight off my soul. You never doubted the miracle or ministry our Savior planned for me and, at every turn, believed that it would come to pass. I love you, my beloved man of valor.

To my young woman of excellence, daughter Mercedes. The day you were born, God gave you to me to be my little sunshine in one of my darkest hours. You are yet shining ever so brightly in mommy's life. During this healing journey, you were there every step of the way, helping me to see the light of Jesus in every experience. Thank you, precious, for continuing to let the Lord speak through you to encourage me to be the best me I can be and to enjoy the beauty that God placed inside. I love you to infinity and beyond!

To all my loved ones and Kingdom of God brothers and sisters, near and far, who came to visit, drove me to appointments, asked the necessary questions to ensure my care team was taking good care of me, texted, inboxed, called with words of encouragement, and gave health advice your love and support was overwhelming. I love each of you and am eternally grateful.

To my health care team of physicians, nurses, and technicians who took such good care of me and made sure we all remained positive, patient, and hopeful. Thank you for your positive outlook and encouragement; you made all the difference in the world during my healing journey.

To my mentor, my friend, my sister, Pastor Shavon Smith. The title and chapter titles of this book are the result of our one-on-one mentoring session. You spoke into my life and ignited a passion to get busy doing my Father's business. Thank you, Pastor Smith, for your obedience to the Lord concerning me and His children all around the world. I love you and hold you near and dear to my heart.

All of you are the support agents God surrounded me with, who spoke life into me in your own unique way! I am eternally grateful for your love and care for me.

Book Sponsorship List

I would like to thank all my sponsors who financially helped birth this work of the Lord so that others might be strengthened. Thank you from the bottom of my heart.

Arizona

Alicia Griffin

CeLeslie Boyer

California

Michelle Beal

Hazel Cotton

Zinda Mitchell

Erlynda Mitchell

Georgia

Danielle Billups

Joni Horne

Patricia Rodgers

Massachusetts

Mercy Myles-Jenkins

Texas

Alicia Woods

Brid'gette Plater

Elizabeth Edwards (3 books)

Eartha C. Demerson (2 books)

North Carolina

Mercedes Bell

Virginia

Myria Thompson

Ohio

Tameka Blalark

New Mexico

Elizabeth Hairston-McBurrows (10 books)

Gary Horton (10 books)

New Mexico COGIC Jurisdiction (5 books)

Michelle Singletary (3 books)

Karissa Culbreath (2 books)

Nina Cooper (2 books)

Daryl Bell

Claude Bell

Paul Archie

Selina Law

Rosalind Jones

Ester Hollis

Sandra Taylor Sawyer

Kia Kennedy

Karla Causey

Sandra Ramzy

Georgina Fourzan

Asia Muhammad

Alvino Sandoval

Etter Houston

Calvin Ward

Rodney Barner

Angela Peaches Russ

Shaunai Blades

Latonya Dawson

Clarice Cregger

Carolyn Foster

Arthur Williams

Gwen Thomas

Ida Archie

Foreword

"I press towards the mark for the prize of the high calling of God in Christ Jesus." - Philippians 3:14

As believers, our deliverance is often seen in our "press." I am often reminded of Job and his press, despite his tribulations and trauma. Job faced tumultuous times and was tested in all areas, yet he never lost his faith in the Lord. He continued to press beyond what he could see and pressed towards that which he believed. After he endured, he was strengthened and was blessed with more than others perceived he had lost. Like Job, we each must shut out all distractions and like the scripture says, press towards the mark of the prize of our higher calling in Christ Jesus (Philippians 3:14, KJV).

The Bible tells us that "Man is born of woman, is of few days and full of trouble" (Job 14:1, NIV). Throughout our lives, we all encounter circumstances we could have never imagined sickness, disease, church hurt, medical diagnosis, family hurt, and the list goes on. It is during these times, where our faith is tested, that we must continue to press, look up, and make a conscious decision to live. It is during these times that we should spend more time with the Lord and ask what He is trying to show us. We must decide for ourselves if we want to give up or if there is more that God has for us to do. I always say that God tests those whom He trusts. When He knows that He can trust us with big battles, then He knows that He can trust us with big blessings. The bigger the battle, the bigger the reward. No battle is without purpose. You must ask yourself, why were you placed into battle.

You must take dominion over anything that comes your way. To take dominion means to boldly subdue and rule over your current circumstances. Do not remain complacent and let your circumstances define you. You must find your identity in the one who created you. This will change your perspective. Then once you have been healed, you must go and strengthen your brother.

Who is it that you are listening to? Are you listening to the voices of others or are you listening to the voice of the Lord and resting in His Word?

We must die to the world and learn to become totally dependent upon the Lord in all things. What you see and hear in the physical is not the final answer. Your final answer is in God's Word. The Bible says that faith comes by hearing and hearing by the Word of God (Romans 10:17, NKJV). Are you tuned in to God? Do you know His voice? It is so important to be in tune with the voice of the Lord and have the gift of discernment when allowing others to speak into your life. Their voice should not overrule the voice of the Lord.

God has given each of us a unique journey, a journey that consists of the good, the bad, and the ugly. However, if we remain steadfast and endure the journey, it is guaranteed to be transformational on many levels. It is in the journey where you get to experience God's grace and mercy. You get to learn about yourself, and you really come to the realization of how strong you are. There is purpose in the transformation, and it is during such times that God can birth things within you that you never imagined. God will use such times to reveal you to yourself, and in the end, He will get all the glory. Sometimes, He must still calm you so that you can slow down and see and hear what He is trying to reveal to you.

Yvette Bell's journey will encourage you to continue in your press. As she shares her story of victory and overcoming that which was designed to steal her joy, your faith will be increased, and you will come to a better understanding that with God, all things are possible. Yvette's transparency and the valuable lessons gained from her experience will encourage you to "Look Up and Live." Remember that you are valuable, loved and that everything you need is already inside you. No matter what the current circumstances may look like, remember that your life has a purpose and that there is a greater calling. There is joy, and life is full of wonderful blessings on the other side!

Let this book encourage you. Let this book bless you. Let this book strengthen you. You are a survivor, and you too can "Look Up and Live!"

Pastor Shavon Smith - Shavon Smith Ministries

Introduction

"I am wonderfully and beautifully made", MARVELOUS ARE THE LORDS WORKS IN ME AND THROUGH ME! I survived for such a season as this. I walk in my newness with great expectations, for I serve a GREAT GOD! I release myself to dream again and LIVE! - Psalms 139:14, NIV, with emphasis

The above affirmation was developed after recovering from chemotherapy, a lumpectomy, ovarian removal, and preparing to enter radiation treatments due to a stage two breast cancer diagnosis. After facing my own mortality, I began to develop a deeper seriousness about completing the work of the Lord. I felt if I had passed from this life into the next, I would have left incomplete assignments on the earth. With the diagnosis, my life goals shifted almost immediately. The experience challenged me emotionally, physically, relationally, and spiritually. I had become comfortable and satisfied with the normality of life and lost the courage to obey God, no matter what. I did not want to stand before my Lord in judgement with my work undone. Had I died, that would have been the case. I am so grateful God healed me completely and extended my life, giving me what I call a "Phase Two" opportunity. It is a chance to represent the Kingdom of God and assist others in their healing journey, as so many have done for me. I am eternally grateful for all that assisted me in my transition and helped me to gain the hope and courage needed to take dominion, in Christ Jesus, over the doctor's diagnosis. According to the King James Version dictionary, taking dominion simply means to have the courage to govern and take control over. In other words, learning how to govern our own life means to have an active role and say in whether each situation impacts us negatively or positively.

To take control over the diagnosis and not let it control me, I began to research many different topics of health and wellness, including how to strengthen my spirit man. I knew my recent urgent determination to obey God needed to be focused with integrity, a great respect of the Lord's call upon my life, and divine revelation of the transition I was experiencing, which is why I enrolled in a virtual Master Class with Pastor Shavon Smith, of New Jersey, Leadership School with Dr. Matthew Stevenson of, Illinois, Deliverance Bootcamp with John Ramirez of New York, Book Writers Bootcamp with Pastor Mercy Myles-Jenkins of Massachusetts, The One Leadership Conference with Pastor John F. Hannah of Illinois, and Apostolic Leadership Training with Apostle Elizabeth Hairston-McBurrows of New Mexico. At the time, I wondered, "WHAT ARE YOU THINKING!" It was a challenge to complete homework assignments for each class on time and keep up with all the instructional times going through therapy. However, as a prophetic intercessor, I needed other proven, God anointed voices in my life that would cause the baby in my womb to leap and come forth. The Holy Spirit of God connected me divinely to each one, and it was up to me to obey the biblical counsel I was receiving.

The ultimate purpose of each training was to be equipped to coach myself and individuals through transition and encourage us to live our lives whole, in great expectation for the manifestation of the greater works of God. I personally experienced additional healing and was challenged to continue to dig deep in my soul, uncovering years of disappointments and unfinished mandates so I can heal and come forth in obedience to God. I received tools to assist in bringing forward the will of

"Look Up and Live"

God for my life. The above affirmation is one of the breakthrough declarations I wrote during this time to assist me in calling forward the completion of assignments.

I am sharing some of the lessons learned and my testimony in this book with you. I believe every one of God's children has experienced their own form of trauma and can overcome anything the devil tried to use to destroy us. We all have been created from the greatness of the creative works of God and deserve to live life in its fullest measure. Nothing that you have experienced is the sum of who you are. I encourage and affirm you, no matter what trauma you have gone through, to trust in our all-powerful and loving God. Know that He will utilize any traumatic experience as a transformative tool to create for you a season of healing. Your testimony will be for the glory of God. He trusts you to tell your story in a way that will honor Him and represent the completed works of His son, Jesus Christ.

My prayer is that everyone who reads this work is transformed through each chapter's spiritual affirmation, as you allow the finishers anointing to complete every good work, He has begun in you (Philippians 1:6, NIV). Therefore, I share with you again the following affirmation. As you read it, declare it in the matchless name of Jesus our Savior until it manifests in your life.

"I am wonderfully and beautifully made," MARVELOUS ARE THE LORDS WORKS IN ME AND THROUGH ME! I survived for such a season as this. I walk in my newness with great expectations, for I serve a GREAT GOD! I release myself to dream again and LIVE! - Psalms 139:14, NIV, with emphasis

Chapter One
Taking Dominion After Diagnosis

Diagnosis - the process of determining by examination the nature and circumstances of a diseased condition, a description that classifies a group...a determining or analysis of the cause or nature of a problem or situation. (https://www.dictionary.com/browse/diagnosis)

All of us have been diagnosed in one way or another all our lives, starting in our mother's womb. Whether by a pediatrician, parent, family member, friend, teacher, co-worker, minister, onlooker, agitator or even at times our own selves. Most of the time what is concluded about us can be incredibly positive. It is in those moments we tend to thrive the most. However, there are seasons in everyone's life that opinions and conclusions about us, whether of truth or speculation, can be extremely hard to hear and deal with. As long as we live, there will be a diagnosis, determination, analysis about us, formed in the good and hard times of our lives. Our mental state (are they sane enough), relationships (do they have the right connections), finances (how much money do they have or not have), ministry (what are we really called or not called to do), education (are we knowledgeable enough), and health (are we healthy enough based on our body type).

Let me give you an example through a portion of my story, in which I have heard diagnosis about me all my life. Some of it may sound familiar to your story. Statistics concluded because I was born into poverty, to unwed parents who were addicted to heroin, I was less likely to succeed. Not to mention not having a consistent home to grow up in as a child, which produced its own set of challenges. As my life shifted into young adulthood, it was interesting to experience those who once cheered me on saying things like; "you can make it," "you are full of promise," "we can't wait to see what you will become," begin to say the total opposite when I became an unwed mother at the age of twenty. They began to make conclusions about my life, that not even I considered. "Once you start having babies, you will end up with many and no one will want to marry you" "you are an aspiring missionary, pregnant out of wedlock, your ministry will not thrive." Then when I graduated from college with a double degree in speech communications and religion, it was said, "she thinks she is better than us." When I married my high school sweetheart, "that won't last long, she will get a divorce," "she is only doing well because she married him, maybe I should get married too." When I became a public official, appointed by the state's first female Hispanic Republican Governor, "she is not Black and not for her community," "she is not a good leader, because she was appointed by a Republican."

So, when I was diagnosed in September of 2019 with stage two breast cancer, I wanted to be sheltered from the diagnosis others might issue. I did not want to tell the story. For a long time, I only told certain ones of the family and asked that they keep the news to themselves. Because I wanted privacy. I did not want to face the judgment that normally comes with traumatic situations in the church, nor the community. Things we often hear when people are facing challenges are; "I wonder what she did to deserve this"? "Is she in sin"? "What evil is she reaping"?

An ever-forming cloud of personal or educated opinions, welcomed or not, will always be present. How we deal with them, when presented to us, will determine whether they will affect our ability to overcome and live our best lives. We can see an example of this curiosity played out in scripture as Jesus' disciples encountered a man blind from his youth in John chapter nine. They immediately concluded sin must have been involved in his physical condition. For surely, no righteous man would suffer such a fate. Many today feel the same way. If a person is in good standing with the Lord, they will not encounter trouble. There is a time when judgement and consequences for ungodly actions are reaped; however, we forget that the Word of God also states,

"Yea, and all that will live godly in Christ Jesus shall suffer persecution." - 2 Timothy 3:12, KJV

"In the world you shall have tribulation: but be of good cheer; I have overcome the world. These things I have spoken to you, that in me you might have peace." - John 16:33, KJV

Because Jesus has already overcome the world, as we continue to lean and depend on His Word, we become overcomers as well. Suffering, especially of a righteous man, is not always due to sin. Often adversity happens just because we are living in this world. As I often say, "life happens." Several circumstances can arrive in our lives at any given time. It is a personal decision, regardless of how we are diagnosed, as to what mindset we will face each persecution.

As Jesus answered His disciples, "neither have this man sinned nor his parents: but that the works of God should be made manifest in him" (John 9:3, KJV). In other words, a witness of the power of God would be shown to others through the healing of this man's eyesight. Generations later, the blind man's encounter with Jesus yet speaks to us, serving as a testament of the power, love, and compassion of Jesus Christ.

God so desires to utilize every adverse situation in our lives as a wit-ness to His glory as well.

> *"For our light and momentary troubles are achieving for us an eternal glory that far outweighs them all."*
> *- 2 Corinthians 4:17, NIV*

Divine Covering

After finding a lump in my right breast, I knew I needed to be examined by a physician, but was currently unemployed, or as I call it on a husband approved extended vacation. Well, just as soon as he allowed the sabbatical from the working world, eight months later my dear husband summoned me back to work. I really was praying for a permanent retirement staycation. We were comfortable financially, to me there was really no need to return to the marketplace. I can laugh about it now but looking back God knew we were going to need the support and gave my husband discernment that it was time to ready our home for not what was, but what would come.

A month prior to receiving an employment offer, a very promising opportunity presented itself. It was what I call a career plateau kind of opportunity. You know that six-figure salary, travel domestically and abroad, while achieving work for the company, where you also build your investment fund and look forward to the day you can finally retire, kind of opportunity. I was at the last round of interviews when I heard the voice of the Lord say, "the Albuquerque Public School District will call and offer you a position, take it". I paused for a moment, wondering why not the other position I so desired, then decided to say yes to the Lord. It was just as the Lord said, within the week, the school district called, and immediately I accepted the position. At the time of my yes, I had no idea why the Lord was directing me in this way. It would all make sense soon.

I discovered the lump just days before new employee orientation late August of 2019. I knew it was not common. I performed self-breast exams often, and given the unusual pain I was feeling, it was something I knew I needed to give immediate attention to. After discovering the lump, God brought to my remembrance a dream I had several weeks earlier. In the dream, I could feel something crawling up my right leg. I looked down to see what it was. It was a snake that appeared to be in attack mode. I remember waking up and entering intercession, rebuking any assignment the enemy was commissioning. At the time of the dream, I was not certain what the specific attack was, but would soon find out.

I scheduled an appointment with a specialist but did not know if my health insurance would cover the costs. I had a form of healthcare, but it was not of any quality and would cover anything major. During new employee orientation, I learned the benefit package included a higher quality of coverage. Praise the Lord! I was also informed the health insurance would be active at the beginning of the next month, just two weeks later. This caused me to be so grateful I obeyed the Lord and did not take the job I thought was best for me. For anyone who has started new employment knows most companies do not activate health insurance that fast. Normally, any new employee would have to be with a company for a probationary period of three to twelve months. Not only that, sick and annual leave would start accumulating almost immediately as well, adding additional hours every pay period, which allowed me to continue to receive full pay while visiting with my care team composed of six different doctors and complete survival therapy (chemo) while working full time. My supervisor was a Jesus-believing Christian. He had patience with my journey and, in a way, walked partially with me through my journey. He also prayed with me and interceded on my behalf. NOBODY BUT GOD COULD DO THIS FOR ME. The other job, which I felt was a better career opportunity, had a heavier workload and would have been more taxing on my time. It would also have not allowed me to take adequate leave that would soon be needed for appointments.

This was a prophetic sign to me that God had set up a divine covering. God was covering me for the journey ahead and showing me, He was right there with me, guiding my healing journey. He proved to me that no matter what, I would be okay. I challenge you to look for the prophetic signs in your life. The evidence of His presence in your life is there. How He divinely works and goes before us to set up a covering and a way of escape (Micah 2:13, KJV, 1 Corinthians 10:13, KJV). When you find the Lord's workings, hold on to them and do not let go. They will serve as your evidence of His love for you and will set a biblical foundation for your journey, allowing you to take courage and dominion over any work of darkness. For what the devil meant for evil, God will always turn it for the good of His children (Genesis 50:20, KJV).

Deciding How to Move Forward

When trauma occurs in our lives, the immediate human response is to begin to ask questions and run a full mental assessment of what has occurred. We can feel overwhelmed and believe we are required to make a variety of decisions. Including, but not limited to, who we should enlist to help us get through, what finances are needed, what resources do we need to inquire, is there pertinent research we need to be knowledgeable about, are there others that may have been through what we are experiencing who can help inform our process, how long do I have to live, should I write a living will? Will I survive this?

Because emergency situations often require quick response, we can forget to start with deciding to settle our mental state of mind. In these times, the enemy would like us to be focused on the things going wrong, not on the healing and redemptive nature of our Abba Father (Romans 8:15, KJV).

It is up to us to decide how we will move forward. Will we keep our eyes and heart tuned into our heavenly Father's will for us or give the enemy space to gain ground by coming into agreement with what is being pronounced over us? Will we forget the healing power of the God we serve and partner with the fear, anxiety, paranoia, doubt, torment, double mindedness, opinions, curses, sicknesses, or diagnosis of the enemy? Or will we press to hold fast to the promises of God, knowing that deliverance is His children's bread (Matthew 15:26, KJV). Because we are His children, we have access to everything at His table and around heaven's throne. Yes, in this world, we will face adversities, but do not forget we are children of the Most High God, and with Him we are already overcomers by way of Calvary's cross. As we look to the cross of Jesus Christ, His sacrifice diminishes any attack of hell or its influence over our lives. During traumatic times we do not see coming, it is a challenge for our humanity to come to this resolve and rest in the promise of healing that flows from Calvary. There are many messages around us in direct opposition to what Christ has completed for us. Even after being diagnosed, I warred many days with what this really meant and knew I needed to settle soon on what my resolve would be. Would I agree with what I heard or was I going to be determined not to give Satan any room to gain a foothold by succumbing to the cancer diagnosis? No matter what traumatic situations we are faced with in life, we all come to this point. After shutting out the noise and sitting in the presence of God to consult with His desire for me, I heard Him very clearly say, "This sickness is not unto death, but for the glory of God, that the Son of God might be glorified thereby" (John11:4, KJV).

After hearing from Him, my declaration became, and yet is, "I have been diagnosed with cancer, I AM NOT CANCER. God is getting the glory from my story"! I had to repeat it repeatedly, until I not only decreed it out of my mouth but believed it in my heart. This is all part of our healing journey and not coming into agreement with the plan of Satan to deliver untimely death when it is not our time to die. Because it was once appointed unto men to live and to die, one day we will face eternity (Hebrews 9:27, KJV). But not today! Deciding to live for as long as God would allow no matter what we are facing, is a decision between us and our God alone. No one else. Not even the enemy can come between us and our maker.

The Healing Process

"Many are the afflictions of the righteous, BUT THE LORD DELIVERS him from them all" - *Psalms 34:19, NIV*

If I am to be one hundred percent transparent and truthful, after the diagnosis, there were days I wondered if I would live to see the next year. The diagnosis of stage two breast cancer, which stemmed from a BRCA1 gene, challenged my sense of mortality. According to the doctors, this discovery placed me at greater risk, because the gene was hereditary. My brother and I grew up with my father's side of the family and were not in a close relationship with my mother. At the time of her passing she started to call and hold long thoughtful conversations with me. I was glad to finally start building some type of relationship, even if it was only by phone. Unknown to me, she was already in treatment for breast cancer. At the time I did not think to ask what stage or strand. I thought cancer was cancer and had no idea there were different types. She let me know that this was a chronic disease women in our family faced for centuries and did not conquer. She lost her battle with breast cancer in 1996 during my senior year of college.

Now twenty-three years later, her story and those female family members who died before her weighed heavy on my mind and heart during the diagnosis phase of my journey. I wondered if I would face the same outcome. Many of you that have been there understand that in a crisis your mind is the first thing you must balance. I had to get to God, my Creator and Lord, and get to Him QUICK or I felt like I was going to lose my mind.

Part of seeking the Lord for divine healing was learning to face my own mortality and rest in the fact that God is yet a miracle worker. This eternal truth does not rest upon what we feel about trials we face on the earth. When our faith is tested in times of uncertainty, it is best not to lean on opinions, but to get back to the truth of the Word of God. Reset a foundation and relearn His heart for His children. I was reminded by the Holy Spirit that this life is not our home and was instructed to refocus on eternity with Christ Jesus. This would be my resting place throughout my survival journey, right next to the still waters of His presence.

Some Christians are living in and teaching only the judgments of God and forget that because Christ came to fulfill the law, we now live in the grace dispensation. Even if we sin, when we repent and turn to God, He throws it in the sea of forgetfulness and brings it up no more (Micah 7:19, KJV). We can be reaffirmed of this eternal truth in His Word.

"Think not that I am come to destroy the law, or the prophets: I am not come to destroy, but to fulfill." - Matthew 5:17, KJV

"The thief comes only to steal and kill and destroy. I came that they may have life and have it abundantly". - John 10:10, ESV

"He will turn again; He will have compassion upon us; He willsubdue our iniquities; and thou wilt cast all their sins into the depths of the sea." - Micah 7:19, KJV

"Christ redeemed us from the curse of the law by becoming a curse for us, we can have victory over sin, shame and darkness (death)." - Galatians 3:13, KJV, with emphasis

"And if the Spirit of him who raised Jesus from the dead is living in you, He who raised Christ from the dead will also give life to your mortal bodies because of His Spirit who lives in you." - Romans 8:11, NIV

Even as we are standing on these truths, age-old questions yet arise. We all have asked them at some time or another. Does God place sickness upon us or Satan? Will God allow the attacks of the enemy to reach us? Since healing is a covenant right for the righteous of God, His "children," why do these things befall us? There appears to be an innate need to determine the nature of a situation or circumstance. Why is it happening, when did it happen, where did it happen, who did it happen with, is it over yet? Curiosity behind the reasons for human suffering seems to become a basic need to know. Because if we can determine or diagnose why we suffer, we may be able to understand better how to overcome and perhaps prevent certain trauma from occurring again. Especially when suffering becomes personal, we want to know how to end it as soon as possible, and in many cases, wish it had never happened.

It is important to remember, that as Christ encouraged His disciples, so does He yet encourage us today. He wants us to know that although in this life we will suffer persecution, we can have peace in knowing, because He has already overcome every trial in this world, we can live as overcomers as well (John 16:33, KJV). If we can shift our mindset to the mind of Christ, and not a defeatist mentality that only looks at the science of a thing, we can stand in the miraculous power of God. For the healing balm of God is yet active in the earth today (Jeremiah 8:22, KJV). He yet delivers, so let us believe in miraclesand not give up on the supernatural intervention of God. Psalm 34:19 will manifest in our daily lives, "Many are the afflictions of the righteous, BUT THE LORD DELIVERS them from THEM ALL."

When we stand on the Word of God, we can move from defeat to victory. We learn to not hesitate to tell of God's healing power, even if we have not yet received the full manifestation of it physically ourselves. Building our faith in God's promises is a courageous stance and helps to shut every legal door the enemy can enter, not just spiritual but also natural. Every door under our control, are the lifestyle habits formed over the years we engage in for pleasure but are not necessarily good for our bodies or health. If we do not learn to shut those doors, we give rights to many diseases and sicknesses. If we are going to heal and take dominion over any form of trauma, as children of God, we will first reaffirm our faith by resetting firm spiritual foundations in God and then get to know the ends and outs of what we are facing.

Taco Bell was one of my favorite fast-food restaurants. I grew fond of their food and would order on a regular basis two to three taco supremes, chicken taco pizza and top off my meal with my must have cinnamon twists. I remember uttering a familiar prayer, "Lord bless this food that it might be a nourishment to my body." He had never responded to my prayer over food before, but this day I heard Him say, "the food you are eating is not healthy and I will not bless unhealthy food to be a nourishment for you." WOW! I was shocked, God basically just told me no, because that is not what He does. I have prayed this prayer for years and eaten all types of unhealthy fast foods. You mean they are not a nourishment to my body? After that I began to learn much more about health and how the body works with what we feed it. Which foods cause inflammation, eventually leading to chronic disease. I learned to shut that door by changing my eating habits. I also learned that stress could send off enzymes in the body, which cause sickness. So, I started figuring out how to destress my life by eliminating stressors that include, but not limited to, listening to or engaging in toxic conversations, not tolerating harmful behaviors, governing thought patterns, getting healed from old soul wounds, and getting plenty of rest. I think I may have overdone the rest part, but I enjoyed being able to silence my atmosphere and be still for a while. Being still gave me an opportunity to learn as much as I could about being in control of my own time, without all the hustle and bustle of life we have all come accustomed to.

Chapter Two
Voices of Influence

There are many competing voices vying for our attention in the world today. Family, friends, strangers, experts, politicians, the enemy, and even our own emotions can gain influence over us in one way or the other. Because what we hear influences our way of life, it is important to guard what voices we allow to speak to us.

As I am writing this book, the world is in the eleventh month of dealing with a worldwide plague that started as the Covid-19 virus in China and has now spread to every nation. There are so many reports on how to conquer the pandemic; however, none has, to date, done so completely. It has affected the health and well-being of all sectors of life, economics, education, mental health, relationships, employment, housing, food, insecurity, and more. In these trying times knowing which voice to trust, for the most accurate information, is vitally important. It could mean the difference between life and death. Filtering through troubling false reports will help us find true guidance that will increase our chances of survival.

As it is in the natural, so it is in the spirit (1 Corinthians 15:46, KJV). In scripture we learn of a noisome pestilence that comes to trouble God's people and how the Lord works on our behalf to ensure we can take dominion over everything that comes to trouble us.

Surely "HE SHALL DELIVER" thee from the snare of the fowler, and from the noisome pestilence." - Psalms 91:3, KJV

According to a post on the Salem Media Groups web-based bible commentary site, pestilence derives "from a word that signifies to speak and speak out. The word "noisome pestilence," is infectious and contagious; it brings a multitude of woes withit to any place or person it comes unto, it is a messenger of woeful fears, sorrows, distractions, terrors, and death itself (https://www.biblestudytools.com/commentaries/treasury-of-david/psalms-91-3.html)". See how destructive words can be if we allow them to infiltrate our soul and move us away from what the Lord's will and purpose is for our lives. At times, it is challenging to move past all the noise of the enemy. To hold the council of the Lord to such high esteem that no matter what words the enemy utilizes to influence us away from our divine inheritance in the Lord, we will not move. "His sheep follow him because they know his voice, but they will never follow a stranger; in fact, they will run away from him because they do not recognize a stranger's voice" (John 10:4,5, NIV).

The blessing is in the joy of knowing the Lord's will for our lives is to deliver us from any destructive plan of the enemy. If we can move past the toxic messages of the enemy and stand on the Word and promises of our God, there is nothing He will not do for His children.

What Did God Say

My greatest hurdle to conquer after the cancer diagnosis was not allowing what I heard to affect the progress of my healing journey. So many negative stimuli about cancer have been delivered through imagery, media, and other means for centuries. Every time we hear the word cancer, we automatically associate it with death. I know, due to the experience of many, cancer has been exalted to be unconquerable. To survive and keep a positive attitude, I challenged myself to find the individuals who lived to tell the story, while praying for the families left to mourn those who passed on. I discovered there are many people whose success has not been widely broadcasted. Many who have lived cancer-free for twenty to thirty years after beating it. I decided that this could be my success story as well. We do not have to receive the negative statistics of those who faced spread or recurrence as our own or let the negativity of the voices of the media influence us to believe any differently. We all have that choice to make for ourselves. Whose report will we believe? If we want to live in the fullness of God's promises for our lives, we will need to choose to stand in His assurances no matter what.

I understand the doctors must inform patients of the odds of their condition and survival, according to their education and research. But I chose to live on the positive side of what I heard. For example, I was told once a woman with the BRCA1 gene is diagnosed with breast cancer, there is a fifteen percent chance it could come back in the same breast or in the other one and a thirty percent chance she will contract ovarian cancer. My response was, and yet is, "I serve a God that can place me in the eighty-five percent of women who do not retract cancer in the breast and the seventy percent of those who do not contract ovarian cancer"! And if any doctor made me feel like there was no hope of the positive side becoming my experience, I shut that door and immediately found a different doctor. This may seem harsh to many, but when your survival is at stake, you will do uncommon things to ensure you form the best care team you could possibly have. Despite popular opinion, we as patients do have choices in what treatment we receive from healthcare professionals.

This would make many believe I was not listening to the doctors. On the contrary, I was taking all their counsel seriously. I just never forgot to compare what I heard from them to what I know God told me, which was, "this sickness is not unto death, but that I might get the glory (John 11:4, KJV), I trust you to give me the glory". Always keep what He told you present in your heart. His words were playing like a record on constant replay. As I continued to hear the advice of all six of my survival care doctors, I finally had a team that was playing to the tune of what God was speaking over me (Zephaniah 3:17, KJV). "You can live, and you will beat this. Take courage my child, look up and live"! They were very encouraging, which is the atmosphere we want. After experiencing their positive care, I began to want this same flow in every area of my life. I found myself longing for the company of people who were willing to help with the healing journey and moving farther away from others who were speaking negatively. I was strengthened by the encouragement, words, and acts of kindness of those who genuinely cared.

Do Your Own Research

We all respect the educated opinions and experience of professionals who have studied and practiced their craft for years. It is important to hear what they say and take their advice seriously. It is also important to know your options, seek second and third opinions, and do your own research. Know what the side effects of the medicines you are prescribed could be. Understand what is involved with surgeries they recommend you undergo. Do not just trust that you are being told everything you need to know. I have found and know countless individuals who have had the same experience. Some physicians do not divulge the intricate details about the process. If I had not done my own research by consulting trusted sources and friends that have gone through similar situations, I would not have discovered preventative therapies, foods that help fight cancer cells, nornatural supplements available to help me heal faster.

In doing my own research, I also found with all the advancements in modern medicine, most cancers are not a death sentence. I am going to repeat that again for all those who may be suffering from this disease or caring for a loved one, "CANCER IS NOT A DEATH SENTENCE." This discovery helped me come to the resolve that with a positive attitude and the right support system speaking life into me, I could fight this seemingly unconquerable giant and win. So, I began to understand although cancer happened to me, I did not have to succumb to cancer controlling me. In other words, I did not have to fear, nor be troubled by it, even hereditary genes are subject to the will of God for our lives.

With this newfound attitude, a desire to discover more about the diagnosis and hereditary gene began to grow. I put my investigative lens on and went to work. I wanted to know specifically what the origin of the cancer diagnosis was. We suffer many things unnecessarily because we will not take time to read further. God said it like this in Hosea 4:6, "My people perish for a lack of knowledge." Many things we suffer can be preventable or its impact lightened with just a little more understanding.

While investigating the origin of the gene, I was asked during a doctor's visit if I was of Jewish ancestry. This was the first time I heard this question. I immediately said not that I know of. My father is Black and mother, to my knowledge, was German and French. The doctor swore up and down that I must be of Jewish descent because the strand of cancer they found in tests is widely known to be the cause of breast and ovarian cancer in the Ashkenazi Jewish population (NIV ELIS, Jewish Telegraphic Agency). Of course, this intrigued me, so I kept on my investigators hat and went digging even further. That Thanksgiving I was discussing with my father what the doctors asked me, and he confirmed that it was correct. He informed me that my great-grandmother on my mother's side of the family was a Jewish immigrant who migrated to the United States.

With each new discovery my curiosity grew, and I desired to know more. I understand that according to the Word of God we know in part and we see in part (I Corinthians 13:9, KJV), the Holy Spirit of the Lord reveals the fullness, and is the only one that can reveal the hidden matters concerning our ancestry. So, I kept looking and found the Jewish lineage my family derives from leads all the way back to Jacob. Yes, I am a descendent of the Jacob of Abraham and Isaac. I was absolutely amazed by this discovery. Only God could reveal this secret thing, I would have never known the root of my lineage, except for the hereditary test due to the diagnosis. This spoke to me prophetically in so many ways and again proved God was with me. There are unique finds in everyone's story. You do not know the jewels you will discover unless you keep digging.

Dispelling the Lies of the Enemy

Traumatic situations in life are meant to paralyze us with fear, doubt, confusion, condemnation, anxiety, paranoia, mistrust, disappointment, regret, judgement, ridicule, deception and more. He wants to blind us so that we would not see God's love and grace for us. The purpose of mistruths the enemy wants to influence us by, is to mute the voice of God, His love, compassion, and instructions for us. If we press to cancel out the lies and allow the truth of God to come alive for us, we can learn to heal and move forward in total freedom.

There are important things to consider when we are looking to silence the lies of the enemy and create a positive, healing atmosphere around us. Here are five points of council the Holy Spirit taught me during my healing journey, that helped dispel or cancel out the swarm of untruths coming at me. Perhaps they can help you or someone you are supporting through a crisis as well.

1. Know the voice of the Lord compared to your voice (emotions) or the voice of the enemy:

The source of the message speaking to us is particularly important to identify. Is this message coming from my own emotions, the Lord, or the enemy? What is the character being represented in the voice directing you? When we can identify the character of God compared to the character of the enemy, we will be able to more clearly know how to cast down council not of the heart of God (2 Corinthians 10:5, KJV).

2. Discern the good intentions of people versus God's intention concerning you:

Although our friends and family love us and want nothing but the best for us, at times their counsel is in direct competition with what the Lord is saying. It is not necessarily false counsel, but their counsel spoken out of their good intentions for us. In these moments it is of utmost importance, that we obey God's directions, no matter what.

3. Discern who can help you from a pure place:

Some nosey Nellie's and negative Susie's, gossipers, accusers, and skeptics would speak untimely death over you. Keep all positive vibes around in your atmosphere as much as possible. You have enough to deal with. Focus on your recovery journey and not the distraction of additional stressors. Positive people will help you discover resources and give advice that will assist you on your journey.

4. Know who can help create positive atmospheres and speak healing over you:

Look around you to discover the people who have great character. People who are encouragers and willing to give of themselves and do not mind you returning the favor if they should need you. Look for those who have been in your life and stayed through the tough times, not those who left.

5. Set up an environment where there are no mixed messages:

Consistent messaging is important and breeds life, laughter, and healing moments. Fill your life with fun activities and hobbies that make you feel good. Spend time with loved ones at locations you enjoy.

Let us continue to remember that Satan is the father of all lies (John 8:44, KJV). He is cunning, seductive, and deceptive and cannot tell you the truth because it is not in him to do so. Look to the truth giver. For He will lead you into all truth (John 16:13, KJV). That is the only way to cancel out the negativity trying to combat your survival.

Governing Emotions

I found myself sitting at the kitchen table early one morning, about two or three o'clock, mentally rehearsing my life. I was very frustrated with my current situation and did not know how to get a hold of the negative thoughts spinning out of control. All the old soul and mind clutter seemed to be so loud, as I was trying to figure a way out. I did not understand why I had to suffer such an illness. I prayed and interceded for peace of mind and before I knew it, I let out a very loud scream. In that moment, I felt like I needed a release, and this was the only way I knew to finally let out all the roller-coaster emotions I was experiencing. My poor husband heard the scream and jumped out of bed wanting to know what was wrong. I guess I frightened him. For him it was startling, but to me it was a way to get a handle on every emotion that was out of control at that moment.

What helps you govern your emotions when they are spinning like a whirlwind? A warm bath, quiet music, crying, talking to a confidant, watching a movie, exercising, reading, sewing, candles? Usually some of these activities work for me. On that day, I felt like I was going to crash under the weight of diagnosis and nothing, but the scream was able to lift the mental load. However, I knew I did not ever want to feel like I had to go there again. I began to pray about other ways to balance and stabilize my emotions in a consistent and permanent way. I recognized the need to not only heal physically, but also mentally and spiritually. And the Lord would give me that opportunity to do so. This illness was my Kairos moment (Greek word meaning opportune time, https://en.wikipedia.org/wiki/Kairos) to not only see the experience at face value, but to look at the sum total of everything I would encounter and let it make me a better person.

It is important to do all we can to get to God. For in our own wisdom, we do not have the ability to break the negative thoughts rooted in our mind, which often give room for the enemy. He will use our words and thoughts against us to create self-defeating prophecies. Our past experiences disappointments, mindsets, doubts, or traumatic memories take up viable and important mental space. If the memories of our past take residence in our cognitive mind, there is little room for the mind of Christ to expand and enlarge in us (Romans 12:2, KJV). It does not matter what we may have been troubled about, if we train ourselves to silence out of control emotions, we can experience so much peace. Our vision, hopes, and dreams will beginto become so much clearer as we can finally hear the transforming and recreating directions of God. He will guide us on how to bring them to pass.

When I came to the resolve that I wanted my whole person healed, the Holy Spirit began to speak to me about the need to be completely made whole by the end of a nine-month period. He said, "I am birthing a newness of life in you. You are going through birthing pains. But when the pain is over, you will have a beautiful new baby. I am strengthening and repositioning you with a new lease on life and opportunities." Now I could understand why such mental warfare accompanied this healing jour ney. Why I had to scream, as a mother in tremendous labor pain. I was not only healing in the natural, but also in the spirit. In a sense, giving birth to a brand new me. Renewed joy, hope, trust in God, love, openness, peace, faith, compassion, understanding, and gratefulness was growing inside of me. God was cleaning my emotions, so that I could have enough room to house and birth new expectations and character.

Chapter Three
Becoming Vulnerable & Transparent

We live in a world where people do not always express their true emotions and rarely let people into their personal space. Especially when dealing with adverse situations. Often, we hide what we are truly dealing with to save ourselves from the judgement of others. What they may say, any perceived condemnation, embarrassment, or regret. We do not want to replay traumatic experiences, because it is as if we are living through it all over again. Many are private, tending to form relationships very loosely and have no desire to let others in too close. Whatever our personal reasons, the difficulty in sharing our story rests on our level of comfort and ability to be vulnerable and transparent.

I remember making the decision not to divulge the cancer diagnosis during the first half of my healing journey to anyone outside of my immediate family. My reasons were the same as others. I wanted to be private until I was ready and willing to be that transparent or vulnerable. There was a point, after much emotional healing had taken place, God questioned me. "If you are not releasing your story because you are concerned about people, you are holding them at higher esteem than me. You have given them a place in your heart where only I should be. They are manipulating and controlling your life from a distance. Repent and place me in my rightful position in your heart. How am I going to get the glory out of your story, if you do not tell your story? I trust you. I know you will give me the glory". He began to remind me of His Word. "They overcome him by the blood of the Lamb and the **"words of their testimony"** (Revelations 12:11, KJV). If we are truthful, most of us have been right here, so private, we move to a position of disobedience, not willing to allow the Lord to utilize our experience for His purpose. We will find that once we begin to obey Him and share our story, a weight is lifted, and we become lighter in our mind and spirit.

Let Help In

As God brought to my attention how closed in I was, I realized this meant I was going to have to reveal my personal needs to others in a way I had not planned or done before. I began to assess who else could I let into this vulnerable and tender part of my life. My husband and I began to discuss how to move forward. We called the extended family together and shared with our church family. I spoke about my healing journey at a women's conference, while streaming live on Facebookand eventually shared pictures of the journey with a broader audience on social media. I will not say it was easy, but once I started to share, I began to feel like a weight had lifted. I also came to understand the true meaning of fellowship and community as seen in the Acts church.

After the ascension of Jesus Christ into heaven, His Apostles were left to lead a nationwide religious reformation. They spent countless hours with Jesus, seeing His miracles, compassion for people, and love for the Father from a close encounter.It was their new charge to lead countless individuals to accept Christ and to teach them of His ways. Believers started forming communities throughout the region to support one another(Acts 2:42-47, KJV). Where there is equal exchange of support and relationship, today's church can safely follow this model. There would be no need to identify who we are able to reveal our humanity to. When a higher level of maturity is present, it is easier to let others into our intimate places to assist us. Not to mention, it was not until I began to share about my situation that a flood of help began to appear. Remember if people are not aware of our situation, they will not know we need support.

Do Not Hide Your Humanity

It is unfortunate that today many people seek for ways to destroy others' character and reputation. These kinds of individuals do not mind embarrassing others by broadcasting their private mistakes or sins. We see this even in the body of Christ, where social media has been utilized to uncover other peoples' indiscretions. Instead of allowing God to manifest and deal with His child, virtual streams are used by some as a platform to ruin ministries, relationships, careers, and lives. Without proper investigation and a prayerful heart to hear what God's will is for that individual, the onlooker often treats them as an outcast, throwing the individual away because they are not able to handle their scars. Most people walk past those they cannot relate to. Setting their face like a flint not to have to deal with the individual's circumstances. Remember the lame man asking for alms at the gate called beautiful (Acts 3:1-11, KJV) and the man beaten, robbed, stripped of his dignity and left for dead along the side of a busy highway (Luke 10:25-37, KJV). In both cases, many passed them by and did not care to assist them in their time of need. Perhaps they did not know how to assist or did not have the resources or maybe the heart to deal with someone else's humanity. It took individuals who had a true heart of compassion, willing to sacrifice their own time, to help someone else find resources and deliverance needed.

Many have forgotten the proverb which calls our attention to grace and mercy. "If it had not been for grace, there go I" (I Corinthians 15:12, KJV). It is important to remember our own humanity. We are not pseudo-Christians who have never made mistakes or will never encounter trouble. To excommunicate people, by not inviting them into brotherly fellowship or helping them in their time of need, is not showing the compassion of Jesus. In all thirty-seven of Christ miracles recorded in the New Testament we witness His love and concern for all people. The believer and non-believer alike. I cannot say I have always had the compassion of Christ to set aside my own needs to help others. However, through this healing journey, Christ showed me that I lacked a greater desire to look past my own situation and see the hurt of another person. As I received treatment, I overheard many stories of those fighting extenuating cases. I was immediately moved to pray for them, instead of myself. After taking time to look outside my own humanity, every environment I would find myself in, church, work, grocery stores, movie theaters, hair salons, and phone conversations, I began to more frequently care for the needs of different people. Before this, living and just surviving in the busyness of life, I did not realize how self-centered I had become. Focusing on myself, had blinded me to the true needs or pain people around me were facing.

We will find the importance of understanding the human condition hidden in our own struggles. As we become more honest about our own downfalls and hurt, we become more open to better understand someone else's challenges. Knowing what it takes to find the courage to survive, helps us connect with people to help them move toward their own healing. When we become free, we can be more open and truthful about what we have experienced without embarrassment, regret, or condemnation. When we are here, in the place of freedom, we can show our scars without hesitation or fear of the opinions or actions of others. By rediscovering our heavenly Father's love for us, it resolidifies who we are in Him. As we stand in His call, nothing that threatens our position in Him, as His children, will be able to move us.

"We are the sons and daughters of the Most High God, a chosen generation, of a royal priesthood, called to show forth the praises of God who called you out of Darkness, into his marvelous light." - I Peter 2:9-12, KJV

Show Your Scars

When people ask you who you are, what do you answer? What information do you give them first? Do you share what you are most proud of, your successes and achievements? Most times, if you think about it, you do not bring forward what we feel is less desirable. Our experiences we are proud of are easier to share freely. In times of crisis, do we operate in this same mentality? Are we able to take off the armor we clothe ourselves with during times of trauma for protection? Can we be transparent enough to uncover the scars gained over the years, so that the Lord can use us for His glory, while mantling us in His supernatural armor? (Ephesians 6:10-12, KJV)

Our scars identify us. They exhibit the painful situations in life we had to suffer through and overcome. The wounds we hide also show the character and wisdom we have gained through learning from our trials. Unfortunately, others cannot fully discover what our true identity is if they cannot see how we have survived our failures and trauma. Thomas, one of Christ's faithful disciples, doubted His resurrection from the dead. He stated he would only believe Christ was alive unless he was able to see and touch His scars for himself. Jesus did not hesitate to call Thomas close and show him His scars as proof of His divine identity (John 20:25-28, KJV).

There is an audience of wounded, doubtful souls wanting to heal, who will recover when they hear your story and can touch your wounded places. They are waiting to see God's character raise up in His children (Romans 8:19, KJV). The hopeless are looking for hope in a day of darkness. We have

"Look Up and Live"

that hope, in Jesus Christ, who is the light of the world. If we hide His light from shining through us, how then can the darkness present in their lives be done away with (expelled). There is life and a new ministry mandate in the willingness to show our scars to others.

It takes courage to allow our story to be utilized by God. We must come to the end of ourselves and trust the will of God. Looking outside of ourselves allows us to see the needs of others around us. In a sense, we are dying to our own desires to be used by God for a greater purpose. Dying to self will birth the will of the Lord in us. Consider Lazarus (John 11:1-45, KJV). Lazarus was not called forth, nor was he or his story widely known, until he died and was in the grave for four days. Everyone around him, including his sisters who had seen the miraculous works of Christ firsthand, lost hope and was overwhelmed with their own sorrow. When Christ called Lazarus forth out of the grave, everyone nearby could not only see the grave clothes he was covered in, but also smelled the four-day stench of death that was on him. Jesus charged those around Lazarus to help him get loose from the clothes. These clothes represented his death. Lazarus was now alive and needed them no more. They had served their purpose. It was now time for him to be reclothed in clean garments.

Even though there are times our scars are very present and visible, we all need people around us who will assist in our deliverance process and help us remove the hurtful after effects of trauma, which were designed to hold us in a state of death. In Christ Jesus, we are no longer dead and have no further need for what bound us in prior seasons. Therefore, we can stand bold in the restoring power of God, with no hesitation about showing our scars in front of other people. We will not hide them, because we understand they show what God has delivered us from and testifies of His goodness.

Yvette Bell

"I am crucified with Christ: nevertheless I live; yet not I, but Christ liveth in me: and the life which I now live in the flesh I live by the faith of the Son of God, who loved me, and gave himself for me." - Galatians 2:20, KJV

Chapter Four
Transformative Trauma

In this healing season, I found myself reassessing life, going back over the goals I set for myself as a youth and young adult. I wanted to know if there was anything else to stay alive for. Had I accomplished everything I had desired, or was there more to do? There was a strong longing to see my daughter advance in her career, form her own family, and help to raise grandchildren in the fear of the Lord. I did not know if this would come to pass or if there were any other career or ministry goals that could be accomplished. Perhaps I was done with writing books, traveling to speak, facilitating workshops, or running conferences. The uncertainty set in, until I began to embrace my healing journey. Instead of fighting to end treatment early, I decided just to go through and look for the newness that would be birthed from the experience. Somewhere along the way, I so longed to take my eyes off the cancer and begin to hope again in the dreams I had for myself and in ministry assignments I knew I had yet to fulfill.

At each new phase of treatment, chemo, lumpectomy, ovary removal surgery, radiation, and lymph node therapy the doctors continued to inform me of the progress my body was making and how it was responding well to the treatment. As they inspected the tissue and lymph nodes removed in the laboratory and found NO SIGNS OF CANCER, the hope I lost for my own dreams began to live again. God proved to me once again, He was with me and what He said to me at the beginning of the journey was in fact true, "this sickness is not unto death, it shall be for my glory. I trust you to tell the story". I could feel my love for God transforming my life right before my eyes. My heart began to have hope again.

All of us have been at the crossroads of life. A place where we question what our future will hold. Is there more to accomplish or are we finished? You know, the seasons of life where we press to find new adventures and things to conquer. When we say to ourselves, I do not want to take my gifts and talents to the grave with me but leave all that I can on the earth for the next generation to glean from. It was both my greatest joy and disappointment to look back to see what I had left undone. Disappointment because I saw the vast amount of work still to be fulfilled. Joy, because it gave me a starting place to pick up where I left off and finish. This new focus proved to me. There were still ministry mandates waiting to come out of me, like this book and others.

As long as we are alive, God will yet pull on us to leave what He has revealed in the earth so that the next generation can glean from it and find the strength they need to fight for their faith in Christ Jesus (Jude 1:3, KJV). Strength to go through all the trials of the end times we are now living in will bring and the faith to continue to share the pure gospel of Jesus Christ. My view on ministry was no longer an in the moment mentality but looked forward to what the needs of the future would be. How can God utilize us to impact future generations, as we encourage them not to lose hope in the gospel because of what they will experience as time waxes worse (2 Timothy 3:13, KJV).

Re-Evaluate Beliefs

If hard times do not cause a person to re-evaluate belief systems, I am not sure what else would. I lost my father while recovering and it was one of the hardest things I had to experience. He was not going to see his baby girl conquer this thing. It tore me apart. I began to recall the conversations we would have about how he wanted freedom from addiction and how he would fight to stay free. The family and I wanted to see him live a prosperous life so desperately, free from addiction. The night of his death, Dad attended bible study, went home, and fell asleep, never to awake on this earth again. I believe God's way of relieving him from the bondage and torment of drugs was to take Dad home while his heart was focused on Him. Why God does not heal some of our loved ones on this earth, that we might see them live free, we may never know.

As I mourned my Father's passing, combined with wondering how much time I had left to live, God began to reveal to me the four ways He heals His children. Consider them and see if they resonate with you:

1. God manifests immediate supernatural healing,
2. God gives strength to endure infirmities and trials until a time of healing comes,
3. God works through modern medicine to heal His children,
4. God gives the strength and ability to endure sickness and hardships until calling His children home to eternal freedom with Him.

Of course, this challenged my interpretation of scripture from teachings about hardship I learned, which became a norm over the years. I found statements like, "if you have faith and a close relationship with God, sickness and trauma will not reach you," to not be the only biblical concept. Scripture tells us that in this world we will suffer persecution, but we can have courage and hope in Christ through it all. Because Jesus conquered the world, we are overcomers of everything in this world as well (John 16:13, KJV). Contrary to the opinions of men, God is with us and will deliver us from hardship, whether in this life or the next, He shall deliver (Psalm 34:19, KJV).

He took me back through scripture to see His love and compassion for His children. To relearn His heart and ways of healing. It did not come easy to me to break free from prior teachings. I began to ask, "why would God allow someone in His will or who believes in Him to suffer or experience untimely death due to genetics." After searching the scripture, I concluded, the way many teach from the Word of God about persecution is often from personal perspective and experiences, which I had difficulty to continue believing in. For when we personally go through hard situations and seek for answers directly from God, He reveals His heart and mind concerning His creation. Oftentimes, what we have learned may not match what we have heard or become accustomed to. So, I have learned to concentrate on what God is doing and saying, for life and death are in His hands alone. We see this in the story of Job as Satan asked to trouble Job in chapter one, God placed a divine limitation on Satan. He informed him that he could touch his possessions, children, and body, but Job's life, he could not touch. Even though it seemed like all was lost, Job was restored more than what he had before.

In the end, even when God allows trouble to enter for our making, or to move us to greater blessings, He will not allow us to be destroyed. His compassion is further stated in John 10:10 of the King James version of scripture, "the thief cometh not, but for to steal, and to kill, and to destroy: I am come that they might have life, and that they might have it more abundantly." God gave us hope in Christ Jesus, not only to live here on earth, but also to live with Him for eternity.

"Look Up and Live"

What Do You Name It?

Reaffirming our faith in the word and ways of God, gives us the courage to rename our journey. No longer waiting on others to define what we are experiencing or how it will turn out for us. Resetting the firm foundation of God's grace and mercy in our heart, re-establishes the boldness we may have lost through years of challenging circumstances. For example, when you hear the words chemotherapy what image comes to mind of the person undertaking this type of treatment? Is it the frail individual that all cancer advertisements depict? Or do you see a person who appears to be healthy? An image where their sickness is not noticeable or known unless they open to you about their experience. The ladder is the type of person I wanted to be. After losing my bodily hair and battling extreme acne from chemo treatments, it took me some time. There did come a day when I heard often, "you do not look like you are sick." I am grateful I finally did not look like what I was going through. It took much work and perseverance to come to this point. I had to enlist the assistance of a friend, who took me shopping for my first wig and eyelashes. I was determined not to look like the images of cancer patients released to the public for sensationalism. I know that God gave me grace and blessed my countenance to reveal His mercy and not my diagnosis.

I decided to declare freedom in the Lord Jesus Christ by starting to rename my journey. Calling it what everyone else termed it to be, did not give me hope. I kept imaging the same images and messaging everyone else sees when hearing of cancer patients. So instead of calling treatment by its clinical name, chemotherapy, I named it "Survival Therapy." Although I did have to continue taking courage day by day and reminding myself of God's promises, this newfound name became my personal declaration and battle cry for the yearlong healing journey I was on. Therapy became my journey to healing, not a resting place nor definition of who I am as a person.

What are you naming your difficult seasons of life? Are you conforming to the perceptions of others or are you rising above any negative words, images or actions being thrown your way? Your perception and hope will follow what you name your experience. If you name it despair, despair will follow you. If the outlook you carry is one of great expectation of joy and peace, then well, joy and peace will find you. We see this concept in the Word of God. "Death and life are in the power of the tongue and they that love it shall eat the fruit thereof" (Proverbs 18:21, KJV). Positive perspective and actions can change your mindset and the environment around you, to be one that is transformative and full of life.

Wearing Diagnosis on the Continence

During the beginning days of diagnosis, I promised myself and family that I would have a survivor's mentality. One that would not give up on life and keep pressing forward, no matter what. If only my demeanor could have resolved to do the same. Early on, I could not figure out how to command my countenance to obey and come in sync with my heart and words. I believe I wore cancer on my shoulder like a dead weight and onmy face like I just ate a sour lemon. I was working full time while taking treatments, and it was wearing me down. Trying to keep up with life around me did not prove to be in favor with me either. I was working many days when I should have been home recovering. I am so glad that before the end of everything I finally learned this lesson. As stated before, I think I got too much rest, if there is such a thing. Until one day, I ran into a stranger that shared a message which changed my whole perspective.

I am not sure who he was; all I know is he could clearly identify I was a cancer patient just by looking at me. He stopped me and without questioning me to verify, spoke with encouragement and authority in his voice. "You will make it through this. Cancer can be conquered." With all the resolve that I could muster up in that moment, I replied, "I know, I am a survivor." Apparently, this was not a suitable answer for him. He started lecturing me about how surviving is not enough. I must learn to thrive and enjoy life. At first, I thought, who is this man to lecture me? He does not know me like that. Then I remembered the text messages I received earlier in the week from two cousins, who live many miles apart. One in California the other in Maryland. The messages stated almost the same exact thing. Do not just survive, LIVE! As soon as I remembered, I turned around to see where the man had gone. I wanted to thank him for the encouragement. Just as quick as he spoke, was as quick as he left, I could not find him. I am not sure if he was an angel sent by God to lift my spirit or not. All I know is a threefold message of hope garnered my attention and according to scripture anything that comes in threes is not easily broken (Ecclesiastes 4:12, KJV).

    I began to do difficult mental, physical, and spiritual work I never had to do before in my life. I did not want my person to exude cancer. I hated even the mention of its name. I even decided not to wear memorabilia with pink ribbons or participate in October's cancer awareness month, which was uncommon for me as a community activist. I always advanced education about the prevention of breast cancer in communities of color. I just did not want to hear about it anymore. I was sure that I would return to supporting the cause one day, but for now I had to concentrate inwardly to find the courage to live. I wanted what my heart felt, my words spoken, and expression exemplified to match. I did not want to carry the spirit of disease nor to be identified by it.

Yvette Bell

Built for Survival

Most of us have learned coping mechanisms throughout our lifetime. Some of them have taught us how to deal with what is wrong, some worked, and others did not. We learned how to deal with problems by avoiding them. We would change our routines, relationships, careers, and even geographical locations not to have to face troubling situations head-on. Most times we revert to what we have become accustomed to escape. We believe this is the proper way of living because it was nor-mal to us and we knew nothing different. In order to transform our lives, we must learn to deal with problems. If we do not face them, nothing will change.

We can change this mentality by deciding to handle every challenging situation, in knowing we were built for survival. Just think about every character in scripture. Each one had challenges to overcome. Adam commissioned to survive by the labor of his hands and the murder of one son by the hands of another. Noah ridiculed because of the task commissioned to him by God to build the ark and warn the people that it would rain and his children taking advantage of his nakedness. Hannah, outcast for not being able to conceive a baby. Paul and the Apostles experienced persecution and many lost their lives for sharing the gospel of Jesus Christ. Jesus Christ Himself was beaten and crucified for His divine love for us. Each one had to posture themselves in the presence of the Lord to find the survivor abilities placed in them by God. If we position ourselves in the presence of the Lord, we can also deal with the deep places of pain. We will find that healing and wholeness is ours, as the Greater One inside of us, strengthens us.

"Look Up and Live"

"I can do all things through him who strengthens me." - Philippians 4:13, KJV

"But you belong to God, my dear children. You have already won a victory over those people because the Spirit who lives in you is greater than the spirit who lives in the world." - I John 4:4, NLT

"That he would grant you, according to the riches of his glory, to be strengthened with might by his Spirit in the inner man." - Ephesians 3:16, KJV

Chapter Five
A Family's Journey

As we walk this journey called life, we are not traveling alone. Our loved ones, friends, co-workers, and sometimes a stranger or two along the way, are willing to share in our life experiences. It is selfish to go through thinking we are the only ones affected by our situation. Every individual will have their own emotions to arise, which will affect everyone differently. It is important not to place your personal expectations on others and meet each person who desires to assist you where they are. I quickly learned that my view of what I should receive from certain individuals, is not necessarily what they were able or willing to give. To eliminate unrealistic expectations, disappointment, and stress, I quickly began to identify who was willing and able to fill certain roles. Oftentimes people felt more comfortable identifying their own role, rather than me or someone else assigning one for them. In doing it this way, others will feel invited to walk the journey with you, in the role they feel most comfortable in.

Have you ever heard the saying, "you need to take care of yourself first, so that you can take care of others"? I have found this statement to be of utmost importance to remember during trying times. Family and friends will also have their own needs and fears as they assist others through trauma. Remind them, as you will also need to remind yourself, that there are resources and support systems for caregivers as well as for the patient. The caregivers focus will be on their loved one and they will often forget about their own needs. Do not let them ignore themselves. They have unique needs and concerns as well. The following is just a brief glimpse into my family's experience, so that you may gain understanding what family members might deal with as they walk with you during your healing journey. For your journey, is their journey as well.

A Spouse's Love

Learning the heart of my husband, partner in life, concerning the diagnosis was important to me. He had almost immediately become my caregiver, a role he did not expect to take on so early in life. After all, we both were only forty-seven years old at the time. My husband's needs, emotions, challenges, ways of supporting, struggles, and growth were all on my mind. He too had his own journey to process. As his wife, who loves him dearly, I really wanted to help him heal his heart. I saw him suffering in silence. I knew he did not want to burden me with his fears of possibly losing me and what that would mean for him and our daughter. But he loved me enough to place his needs secondary. My healing and survival were his priority. He often let me know that when he felt helpless, feeling there was nothing he could do to help me or be by my side, prayer was his place of comfort.

I can hear him now encouraging me to fight to live. In the times of great pain and mental discouragement, he never gave up on hope. He always knew that I would live. His greatest need was for me to believe as he did. You know how people say that others were their greatest cheerleader? I will not say that. I will, however, say that he was a very tough coach. You know how they stretch you and push you to do things you never thought you could do? And in doing so, the player is not always happy with the coach? Sometimes the player feels the coach is unreasonable and pushing too hard. But all along, the coach sees the potential in the player and is just trying to help the player see it for themselves so they can walk in it? Well, that was my husband, and I have to say he was right. There was strength in me that I had no clue was there. As he kept encouraging me, strength unknowingly appeared out of nowhere. And suddenly, I could see my future clear. I had hope again.

My husband is a man of many talents and hobbies. A little-known fact about him, only close family and friends will know, he loves to make candles. He is so particular on what type of scent, color, wick, wax, and container to use. He will spend hours, and sometimes days, to find just the right contents. Sometimes he brings me along with him. I just love to see him create his masterpieces. The candles are sitting around the house in very peculiar places. We light them mostly during the holidays. He also loves to work on cars. If I let him, he will spend all his free Saturdays in the garage fixing up old classics. He is mostly known for his musicianship and kind spirit. When churches around the area need assistance, if available, he is willing to help. I have watched him over the years as he gave of himself so willingly. Toward the end of everything, I asked him how he felt now that we were almost done with treatments. He so gently told me that he was ready to start doing some of the things we put on hold. Like hobbies, travel, visiting with friends and family, ministry assignments, and working on his cars. He stated that he is ready to live again.

A Daughters Encouragement

I was told before survival therapy (chemo) began, I would lose my hair the second week into care, which was one of the side effects I dreaded the most. I spent the past three years growing a head full of beautiful, thick, curly, honey blonde, natural hair. This would be such a loss to me, so I held on to hope that God would let me keep my hair. I was already losing so much; at least He could do this one thing for me. So, I decided to help Him out. I called myself applying a deep conditioner to really make sure my hair had as much moisture as possible. I had no clue that the product, when mixed with the chemicals in the medicines I was taking, would fuse my hair together. Yes, that is right, fuse my beautiful hair together! Here I am with clumps of hair that would not separate, no matter what I tried. I cried like a baby and questioned God as the tears flowed down my face. I said to him, "God, I thought you were going to let me keep my hair? How could you let this happen"? He answered so kindly, but so stern, "I never told you I was going tosave your hair; that was your desire." WOW, that was a wake-upcall. Sometimes we can trust God so deeply for something we want, till we mistake our desire for His. I began to reach out toa friend who owns a hair salon, she tried to help me untangle my hair. I mean she really tried. Eventually within the span of one week, I had to plan a shaving party to cut it all off. Since childhood I always had long thick hair, I was not used to having no hair. I mean, I was beside myself and in the early stages of depression, not only about my hair, but overall self-image.

The first time I wore a head wrap in public, which I had never done, was during a Sunday church service. Now those who know the Black church and how we adorn ourselves with outer apparel, know that to do something unfamiliar and uncommon on a Sunday is very unusual. We dress to the tee. I struggled to put an outfit together and was late to church. So, on the way I took the time to call my baby girl. I reached out because I needed her to talk me into the courage needed to face the day with boldness. I can still remember her words to me as if she uttered them today. "Mom, this is your opportunity to rediscover the inner beauty that you have forgotten you have andto find new beauty within you."

My daughter's words of encouragement throughout this journey were always so powerful, but for some reason the words she spoke this day were different. They awakened a part of me that had long been hidden. Those words were prophetic and called life to me in a way that I had not heard spoken concerning me for some time. I had long lost myself due to other traumatic experiences years prior, which had nothing to do with my outer self. I made some missteps in life, which I am grateful that the Lord allowed me to repent and correct my path with Him and with people. During that season, I let others tell me who I was or was not. That day I remembered the scripture I would teach other women. It used to be my personal battle cry against the enemy's plan to destroy my life. I loved it so much, until I taught other women to declare the truths in scripture. Somehow, due to many traumatic life experiences, I let go of its truths. It was time for me to return to my identity and live in healing and wholeness. There was still hidden beauty in me. I just had to rediscover it.

"I will praise thee; for I am fearfully and wonderfully made marvelous are thy works; and that my soul knoweth right well." - Psalms 139:14, KJV

As I was learning to overcome my own insecurities, I soon found out that I had passed some of them on to my baby girl. After all treatments were over and we were informed I was now in survivorship care, she shared the following insert from her personal journal with me. I would like to share it with you, because it is the heart of a child and exemplifies a small portion of what they experience watching a parent endure hardship.

On June 2, 2020 Mercedes wrote in her journal the following and titled it "Insecurities".

"Look Up and Live"

It seems toward the end of 2019 and the beginning of 2020 my life has been a huge test. In September, I found out my mother was diagnosed with stage two-breast cancer. I still remember how my body trembled as I heard my father tell me over the phone as I was sitting with my Pastor and First Lady privately in the church house (Pastor Travis and Lady Anselita Newkirk). My grandfather died suddenly in February and then shortly after I experienced another failed relationship.

In addition to all of this, I am now living through my first pandemic with COVID-19, and our nation continues to cry out as George Floyd was murdered by the same people we assumed would protect us. Amid everything happening, I am trying to maintain my sanity while focusing on my personal and spiritual growth and securing my financial future. During quarantine, I have invested in stock, bought a new car, registered for an online Spanish course, applied for my first credit card, and I am planning to purchase a home by October. My mind was in a million places at once.

About three days ago I vomited for the very first time. Yes, the first time in my life. I was eating some of my homemade queso and started watching wedding videos. In the middle of me watching, I thought about my grandfather not being present when I am to marry one day. Teary eyes became tears, which turned into a good cry, and morphed into a pitiful weep. I began to cough, choke, and then bam! There went my lunch. I started dealing with fatigue and some minor chills. My temperature hit ninety-nine and I automatically thought, "Corona." My mom ended up telling me that people say, "you make yourself sick when you stress yourself out." I guess I was dealing with a lot more stress than I realized.

Speaking of stress, let me circle back to what this chapter is about, "insecurities." As I spend a lot of time at home, I am discovering I have A LOT of those. Now, do not get me wrong,

I am in a better place than I was a year ago. The older I get the more "so what" is written across my face, when it pertains to anyone having a problem with me being my genuine self.

Today, I had taken a beautiful picture of my mother and I laughing via Facebook video. Her hair has grown out beautifully. Her curls naturally sway, and her baby hairs look like they took hours to perfect when all she did was put oil on them. It is at the "Halle Berry" shortcut stage. It suits her well and I love how it amplifies her defined cheekbones. She is a walking marvel. However, when I stated that I might post the picture, her struggle showed its ugly head. She did not like it. She began to talk about herself negatively. I quickly got irritated. Not only was she beautiful, but also this was a special moment that I wanted to share, and I could not do it. I did not want to go against my mother's wishes.

No matter how upset I may have felt in that moment, I had no right to allow it to linger because this is something that has been passed down to me as well. To ensure the flaws I hate about myself do not go on display, I continuously retake photos to get the right lighting, angle, and crop before I post on social media. There was one photo posted on Instagram several months before, where I was comfortable enough to show my acne and acne scars to my audience. But that was a rare occasion.

Insecurities are bondage. When you allow them to take control, they snatch a part of your expressive freedom. You mute your expression of style, personality, and even faith. Insecurities partner with death. Being free from this type of bondage, allows yourself to experience who you truly are without boundaries.

Extended Family

As we go through life, we tend to forget about all those around us who care and love us most. There are times that we do not notice they are there and forget to call or visit. Our hectic schedules often keep us engaged in other matters. It is not until we are forced to slow down, we look around us to see who stayed with us past the hard times in life. Because it is those who stayed, and did not leave, we can count on the most. I can admit, the busyness of my former schedule caused me not to see the plethora of loved ones present in my life. God opened my eyes to His love for me, He began to show me everyone who loved me as well. He even created divine connections with new networks along the way.

I really did not want to tell anyone of what I was going through. When I finally decided it was time to inform the extended family of the diagnosis and all I would have to endure in the days ahead, the Lord gave me to set up a conference call. He knew, at the time I was in no mental condition to call each of them one by one. To do that I would have had to repeat everything and answer individual questions. This way, we could inform and answer questions at one time. It was hard for me to communicate my true feelings, my husband had to take over. I remember so much encouragement flowing through the phone, not just for me, but for one another. My cousin sang a song to lift my spirits. A song we know from the church with the words, "Walk with me Lord, while I am on this tedious journey, walk with me Lord, walk with me." I would have missed out on such a precious moment with family, if I would have kept the diagnosis to myself.

You already learned in an earlier chapter how God set my career path to land at the Albuquerque Public School District, to be surrounded by a supervisor and co-workers who would speak positive words to me and care for me as I worked full time, while going through treatment. God also connected me with small business owners and a host of community and ministry leaders, who would hold our family's hand to pray for us and provide resources that were desperately needed.

God will divinely work on our behalf to give us connections and an extended family we did not know existed. Stay open to whatever it is God wants to do in you and through you. We are unaware of where our journey will lead us and who is waiting on the other end. What God does, He does well. We are the ones closed in and unwilling to form new relationships, because we are comfortable with the circle that we have formed. When we allow the Lord to break the circle to let others in, we will find individuals who will enrich our lives with so much newness, resources, and positivity.

Church Family

My church involvement took on a whole new meaning for me as I evaluated if I had the strength in my body to remain a faithful member. The various church services I would attend in times past, I could not always be present. But when I was well enough to participate, everyone was so encouraging. It felt like I had a church family who was trusting God for me and genuinely cared about my well-being. They held onto faith and were persevering in prayer on my behalf. They believed that the healing power of God would manifest, and it did show up. This reminded me of the support system of the New Testament church. Whatever was needed for the widow, orphan, hungry, homeless, and the feeble-minded, the church would pull together andmake sure every need was met.

Our world needs the church to be an extended support system for families. As Jesus Christ was our great example. He cared for all humanity, the well-being of the believer and non-believer alike were important to Him. Often feeding the hungry, raising the dead, healing the sick, and casting out tormenting spirits. His main concern for people was that they be free enough to receive the love of His heavenly Father. When His heart and mind for us is evident in a church fellowship, renewed love and trust can be ours as He transforms our situations.

Chapter Six
Our Story, God's Glory

Your life story matters and is uniquely yours. No one else has experienced your journey but you, you are the expert of your own challenges. Only you know the intimate details of every minute of your process. The emotions you have experienced, thoughts you had, physical pain endured, relationships challenged, financial needs discovered, how you pressed to find hope, sleepless nights encountered and MUCH MORE. Others will tell your story for you, through a secondhand lens, which is always incomplete. So, we might as well allow God to utilize us in expressing the intimate places of our own stories. The passion you exhibit while sharing with others will resonate with the heart and assist them in overcoming whatever they may find difficult. Many will celebrate your journey with you because it will sound familiar to something they have had to conquer. Become comfortable telling your own story with boldness and authority in Christ Jesus. You are the only expert of your life's story. You have always lived the main role, front and center. Others are bystanders, looking in.

Your Story Will Minister

After God's direction to share my story, so He can get the glory, I often asked myself, "Who would be interested in my story? Who will listen? Does my story even matter"? My understanding of the relevance of what I experienced was not the same of God's mind or heart for me. Scripture tells us that our mind is not His, He has ways that we would not even consider (Isaiah 55:8, KJV). He even reshapes the foolish things of this world and confounds us by how He utilizes that which we think is no longer usable.

One of my good friends would meet with me every Monday to give me resources, encouragement, and stories of those who survived cancer. She believed the survival stories would help me gain hope. I never imagined how important it was to hear testimonies from individuals who conquered what you are challenged with. But, as I searched for those survival stories and listened with an open heart, my perspective shifted. I began to tell God, if you can do for others, surely you can do it for me. Many of the stories I heard were of individuals depending on eastern medicines for healing. The individuals report the cancer left and did not return. So SURELY, our God who has all power and authority over everything in the earth can heal me. For He is bigger and greater than all other forms of medicine. He is yet our great physician (Jeremiah 8:22, KJV). If we continue to exalt Him for who He is, He will show and reveal His greatness.

Just as I searched for survival stories, so will someone, one day, search for mine. And my friend, trust me they will search for yours as well. People desire your story. Tell it from a grateful heart. I found as I was willing to open up, I even talked to strangers about the Lord's healing power. There was a new ministry assignment, anointing, and authority in Christ forming. The more we make ourselves available to God, He will utilize us in many ways. It does not have to be among crowds of people, and some may have that experience. Either way look for Him to use your newfound boldness in Him daily. In phone conversations, through prayer, talking with family and friends, in your community, shopping for groceries, during doctor's visits, a willing heart can be utilized anywhere at any time to share the goodness of the Lord. People are waiting to experience God. You have Him. Let Him work through you.

Our story not only blesses others, each time we release it, a boldness to continue telling the story develops. And as Revelations 12:11, NIV, states, "They triumphed over him by the blood of the Lamb and by the word of their testimony; they did not love their lives so much as to shrink from death." You are an overcomer over every plan of the enemy, who would have you to shy away from testifying about the love of God. But tell about His mercy and grace anyway and push the enemy of your soul back. Although our stories are not for everyone, they are for someone. Find that someone and do not shy away from allowing what God has done for you to bless others.

Telling your Story, Reveals God's Glory

Becoming comfortable sharing some of the intimate information of how we experienced God's presence with us, helps us to always point all our experiences back to Christ and to trust, obey, and worship Him NO MATTER WHAT! Paul is an example of going through great trials and yet redirecting the attention of others back to the praises of God. He even reminded those who questioned his character, despite what he had to endure, his boasting would always be in the Lord Jesus Christ. Read of Paul's suffering below and discover how he always lifted Jesus despite the hardships he faced. He told of his suffering, but never neglected to glorify God when telling his story.

"Look Up and Live"

"Five times I received from the Jews the forty lashes minus one. Three times I was beaten with rods, once I was pelted with stones, three times I was shipwrecked, I spent a night and a day in the open sea, I have been constantly on the move. I have been in danger from rivers, in danger from bandits, in danger from my fellow Jews, in danger from Gentiles; in danger in the city, in danger in the country, in danger at sea; and in danger from false believers. I have labored and toiled and have often gone without sleep; I have known hunger and thirst and have often gone without food; I have been cold and naked. Besides everything else, I face daily the pressure of my concern for all the churches. Who is weak, and I do not feel weak? Who is led into sin, and I do not inwardly burn? If I must boast, I will boast of the things that show my weakness. The God and Father of the Lord Jesus, who is to be praised forever." - 2 Corinthians 11:23-31, NIV

I am not saying we should be okay with suffering trauma; God forbid. Nor am I suggesting the only time God will be with us is when tribulation is present. However, having God's glory, or by definition, the beauty of His power and authority with us when we do tell of His goodness, is like none other. His Lordship rules over all in the earth and will orchestrate everything to the good of those who love Him and do His will (Romans 8:28, KJV).

I remember traveling to my mother's funeral in California at the age of twenty-four. I was sitting on the plane confused as to why the Lord would allow me to reconnect with her, only to take her soon after. Just as any child who grows up with their mother or father absent, I always longed to have her in my life. I began to read from David's Psalms and came across a scripture that has been my strength during great trials ever since. Perhaps you can find hope within it as well. In Psalm 119:71, David says when he suffered, he came to know the ways of the Lord.

In other words, he rested in the fact the Lord was with Him and His ways governed his life. The closer we get to God to hear His will for our lives, the more we can help others lift Him above all situations in their lives. When the beauty of His presence shows up, everything is subject to the power and majesty of God. Scripture tells us that His glory is present in the wholeearth. So, if it is present on the earth, it is already here waiting on us to place a demand on it. Your testimony is a form of demand. Tell your story and watch the glory of God show up.

Where to Tell the Story

Would we hide the light of Jesus? Since His glory shines through our story, then why reserve it for only a few or certain audiences. When the Lord's miraculous healing power manifests, we should want to tell everybody. I remember lying in bedone morning, feeling so depressed over what was happening tome. I was not in any position to share the goodness of the Lord and I knew it. I heard Jesus say just as plain as day, "If anyone is ashamed of me and my message, the Son of Man will be ashamed of that person when He returns in His glory and in the glory of the Father and the holy angels (Luke 9:26, NLV)." I did not want to be disowned before God. So, I got busy thinking of every place I could share about the healing power of God.

After the first round of survival therapy, the lump in my breast and the one in the lymph node was gone. I could no longer feel them. I did not say anything to anyone except my husband just in case I was wrong. I wanted my doctor to verify whether this was the case or not before declaring a miracle. As I was getting dressed to go to the doctor, I heard clear direction from the Lord. He wanted me to tell the doctor, God uses modern medicine to create miracles that heal His children. Now as many times as I visited health care professionals during my thenforty-seven years of life, I never heard anything like this.

God basically, instructed me to march into the examination room and declare a miracle. So, with my newfound determination to obey God, I sat down and declared what God instructed me to proclaim. The doctor quietly started digging to try and find the lumps that were clearly there before treatment. After careful examination and taking her time to contemplate what she just experienced, she stated, "God does use modern medicine to heal His children, and this is a miracle!"

Imagine the excitement and gratefulness that flooded my soul. I immediately started a mental listing of everyone I could share the miracle God gave me. All the usual individuals came to mind: family, friends, and my church. However, since God had done this great thing for me, I wanted to open the floodgates of my heart and share it with whoever would listen. For perhaps they too needed to know and be reaffirmed of the fact that God is yet performing miracles.

You too can think of additional ways you can share your testimony. On social media, with other doctors, nurses, other patients, co-workers, in workshops, speaking engagements, speak of God's goodness everywhere you have an open door. Let the floodgates of gratefulness flow freely. Do not allow your voice to be muted any longer. There is a desperate need for our Savior's power to be known more widely on the earth.

Chapter Seven
Look Up and Live

Living in dominion over any diagnosis takes courage and intentional effort. In moments trauma threatens our life or well-being, choosing to live a full and happy life becomes easier said than done. Standing in healing is not as simple as it appears to be. But you can do it! Choose to stand in the promises of God, who will never give up on you. As long as you are alive, you have much life to live. God's heart's desire for you, is that your hopes and dreams come back to life. Consider the following scripture. "At least there is hope for a tree: If it is cut down, it will sprout again, and its new shoots will not fail. Its roots may grow old in the ground and its stump die in the soil, yet at the scent of water it will bud and put forth shoots like a plant (Job 14:7-9, NIV)." If there is hope for a tree to live again, surely our heavenly Father's love for His children will water every one of our traumatic situations and cause new life to come forth.

Receiving the True, Pure Love of Christ

"For God so loved the world that He gave His only begotten son, that whosoever believeth on Him should not perish, but have everlasting life". - John 3:16, KJV

Learning how to rename your journey according to God's heart for us depends upon us being able to receive the pure love of Jesus Christ. His love is not known or displayed according to the ways of this world. For the definition of love is different, depending on who you speak to. Each of our lived experiences are different and hold within them differing perceptions and opinions about what love is. Some have a distorted and toxic way of loving others. This way is filled with lies, bitterness, control, offense, hurt, unforgiveness, ill words, and unkind actions. The true pure love that flows from our Father's heart is full of compassion and forgiveness. Our Father's love seeks to give His children eternal life and exhibits compassion, grace, and mercy. At times chastisement and correction, which according to the scripture is what loving fathers do for children they love. God's love will correct us so that we remain close to Him (Proverbs 3:12, KJV). It is not a harsh kind of tough love that the world has come to define His correction as.

Embracing the true love of God, means that we long to be with Him. Even if it means leaving all that is in this world to spend eternity with Him. Just think about it, if we truly were living in the fullness of God's love for us, we would long to be in His presence more than we desire to do anything else on this earth. There is so much vying for our attention, television, sporting events, concerts, family gatherings, entertainment venues, vacations, and often church activities. We crowd our schedules with so much till we do not schedule in time to sit with the Lord. After experiencing trauma and being literally sat down in His presence, I realized how tremendously jam-packed my life was in the prior season. Ripping and running trying to keep up with the cares of this world, I did not have room to receive a fuller measure of His promises.

Although I was not comfortable with the sickness, I became grateful for the carved-out time God allotted me. It allowed me a quiet space to spend more time in His presence to refocus and shed many cares of the world. I could now see more of the supernatural ways of God, where I was reminded not to place all my hope on what I could see with my natural eyes. He is an eternal God who works in ways we cannot fully understand. During this time, a song written by Michael W. Smith entitled, "Open the eyes of my heart Lord", became a regular worship song during times of devotion. As my spiritual sight improved, I could see Christ more clearly, He is my eternal hope of glory. My focus was no longer on the diagnosis, but on my Savior's love for me!

Break Agreement with Death

Agreeing with death means that we have settled on its facts and existence in a way that aligns us in harmony with it. We begin to tolerate it and accept its reality. Unknowingly to me, fearing death, invited a spirit into my home. Our unwillingness to fight for life, unbeknownst to us, is a decision to give into death. If we do not persevere to do the things it takes to help extend life, we have in a sense come into agreement with untimely death. For, our emotions and thoughts are often revealed in our actions.

We hear from God in different ways. Dreams, open visions, His written word, sermon, prophecy, prophetic signs, or directly from Him. I was sitting in my living room one day and I could see a dark image sitting in the corner. The Lord immediately let me know it was the spirit of death and that is all He said. I did not know if it was my time to go or not. Of course, I prayed that it would leave, and it did not go anywhere at first. I told my sister-in-law what I saw and heard. She immediately told me to pray against untimely, premature death. I began to do that, and it left immediately. Although I appreciated the fact that the spirit was gone, I wanted to know how it got into my home so that the spiritual door it entered through could be sealed off for no return.

I believe God was showing me that I gave death a legal right to access my house and environment. To ensure it did not come back, I had to transition my state of mind, that I would no longer come into agreement with death. To break the mental covenant I made, it was vital I agreed with what God was saying, in order to implement what I learned about how the body works. To be a good steward over my body I must continue:

- exercising,
- eating healthy foods,
- doing more research,
- let people help me,
- stay current with treatments,
- keep my life distressed, and
- keep laughing.

All these actions are examples of how to break agreement with premature death. In taking these actions, we not only do this for ourselves, but we model healthy behaviors for generations to come.

The Life Giver

After enduring a year-long process of treatments, I finally heard the words, "you are now entering survivorship care," which is how doctors now refer to remission. Hearing these words gave me great joy. This meant that there is no longer any sign of cancer cells in my body. However, there were lingering after-effects from all the harsh medicine that was prescribed. I thought that once I was done, I would be truly DONE! But it was now time to rebuild my body and deal with minor conditions created during treatment. They were ever-present reminders of what could happen if I did not stay diligent with the follow-up visits that were to come.

Yvette Bell

Every day I strive to remind myself that our Savior was crucified on the cross to give us eternal life with our Father in heaven. His sole purpose of coming to the earth and rising with all power and authority, was so that we do not have to die an eternal death but be reconnected with our heavenly Father. Christ has given us that same authority over death and darkness when we receive Him into our hearts and become sons of God.

> *"Because you are his sons, God sent the Spirit of His Son into our hearts, the Spirit who calls out, Abba, Father. So, you are no longer a slave, but God's child; and since you are His child, God has made you also an heir."* - Galatians 4:6-7, NIV

We serve the life-giver, for He has come that we might have life and life more abundantly (John 10:10, KJV). In otherwords, we have a choice to step into what was already promisedto us, a full life in Christ Jesus. He has already given us a glimpse of hope along the way to build up our faith that He is with us and desire that we live full lives. We are released by the Holy Spirit of Truth to live and take dominion in Christ Jesus over every diagnosis, the enemy sent to try and destroy us or our loved ones.

> *"This sickness is not unto death, but for the glory of God, that the Son of God might be glorified thereby."* - John 11:4, KJV

Encouraging yourself is not a one-time occurrence. It is not even a daily exercise, but a lifelong task. As long as we live in this world, there will be things to overcome and remind us of the hard times. We can take courage in knowing we serve a God that will restore. You may have lost some things; your health, loved ones, or possessions, but you still have so much more to gain. Do not waste your energy worried about how your future will turn out. When we place our trust in Jesus, He will help us complete everything we need to complete, nothing shall be lost. Make a commitment today to choose to live and be determined to stay the course. Do not let anything detour you from enjoying your life nor cause you to live with your head hung down in despair. For God is our protector, glory, and strength. "But thou, O Lord, art a shield for me; my glory, and the lifter up of mine head (Psalms 3:3, KJV)."

Accept your new life in Christ today and receive the newness that only comes from Him, "Behold, He makes all things new (Revelation 1:5, NKJV)." So, in Him you can declare, "This enemy I shall see no more," with great expectation that the Lord will meet you at your point of faith in Him. No matter what you must face in this life, never lose your hope and trust in the Lord. Always resolve within yourself, that although challenges may come, and at times circumstances seem uncertain, you will not give up on God, but choose to look up to Him and live!

Yvette Bell

Healing Journey in Pictures

October 2019

Port Placement, First Day of Survival Therapy (Chemo), Hair Loss Due to Therapy and Shaving Party

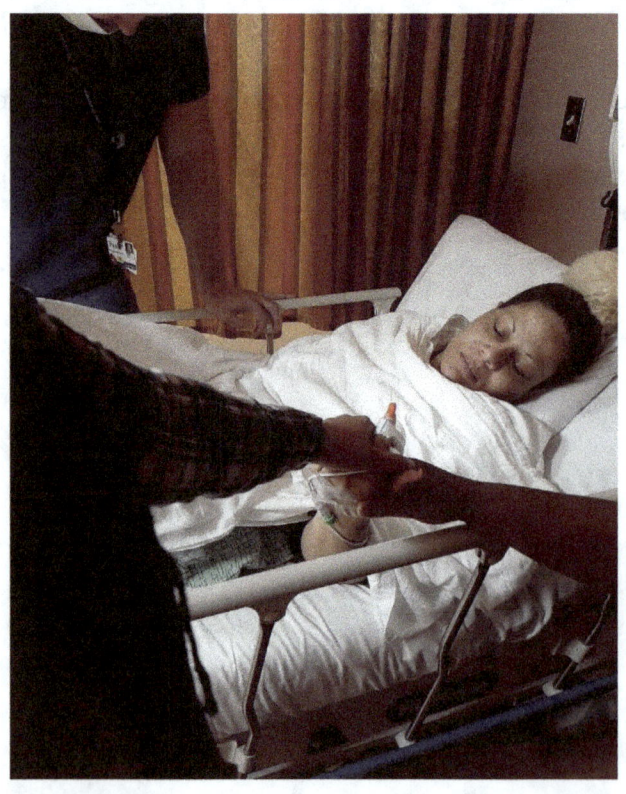

"Look Up and Live"

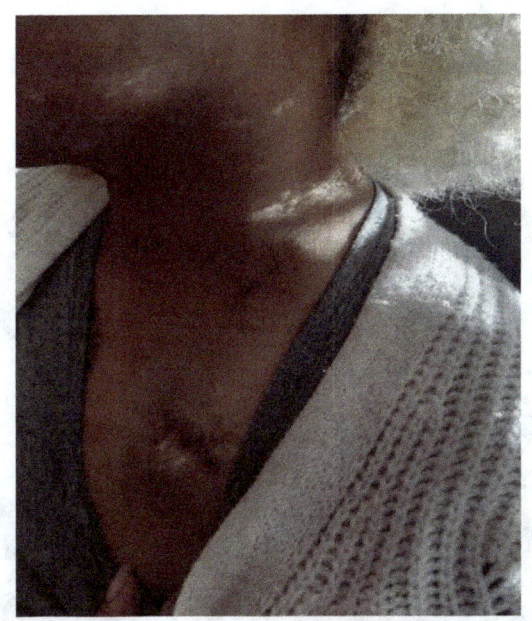

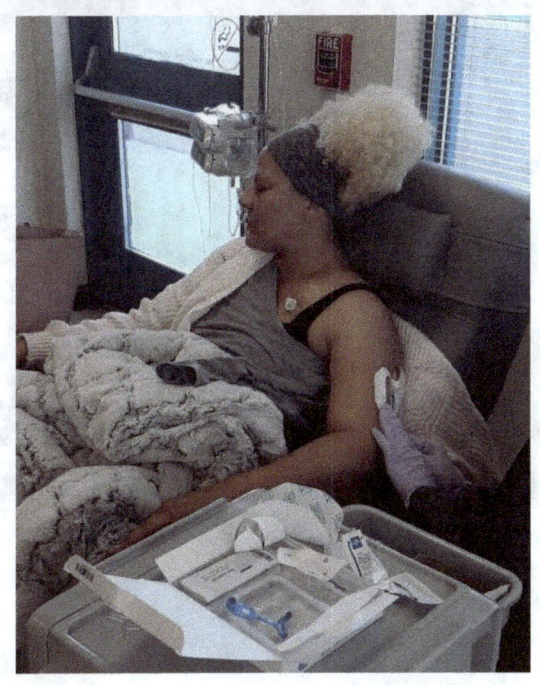

Yvette Bell

"Look Up and Live"

Yvette Bell

"Look Up and Live"

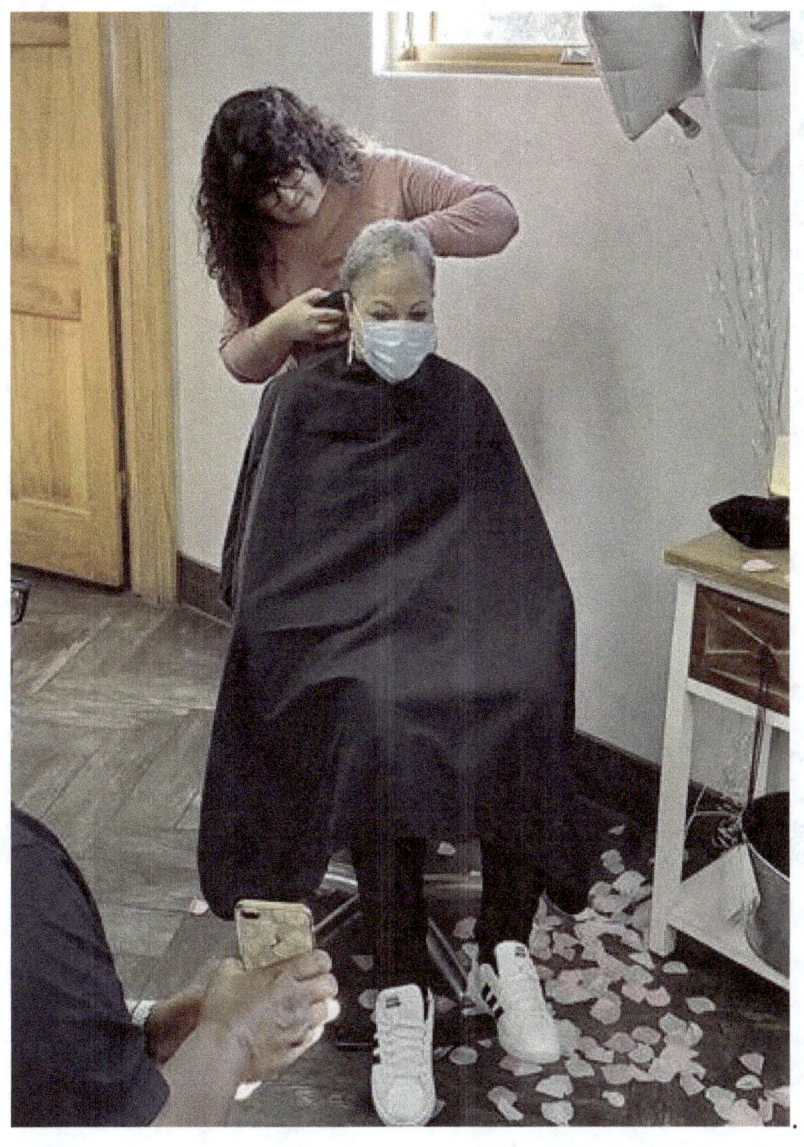

Yvette Bell

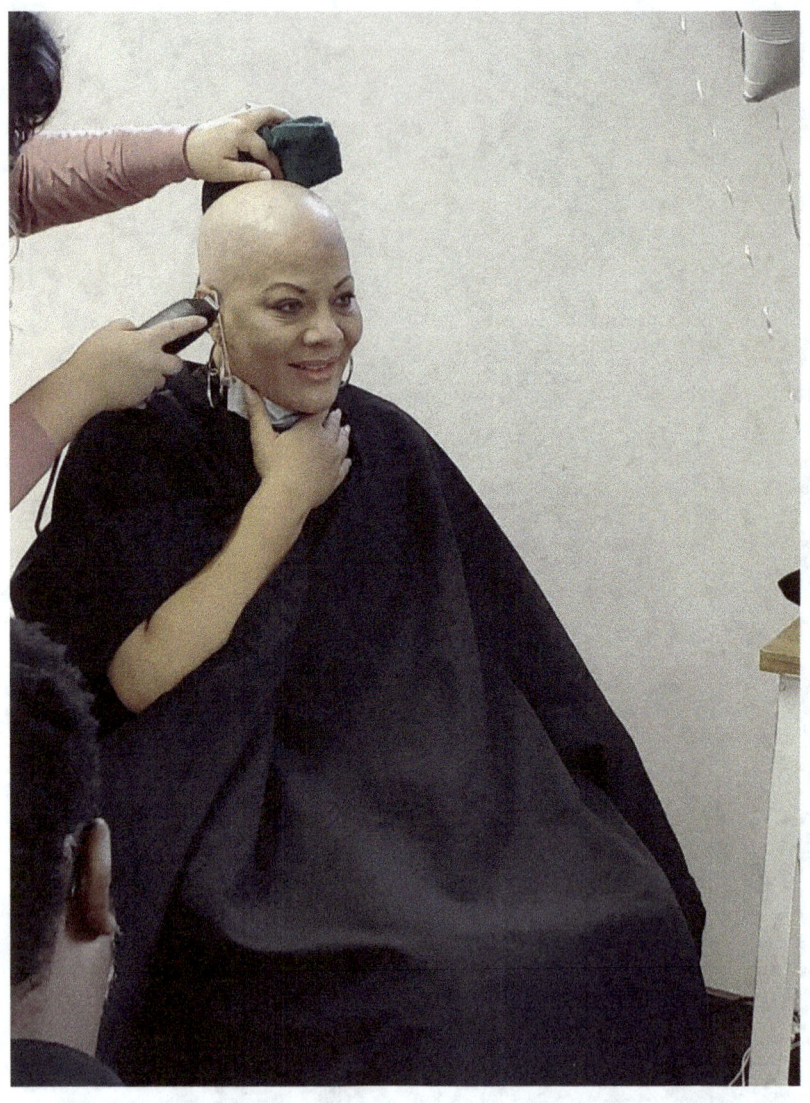

"Look Up and Live"

November 2019 - February 2020

Extreme acne and skin darkening due to treatment, working hard to improve emotions and self-image, wearing a wig and eyelashes for the first time then deciding to go natural as hair grew back out.

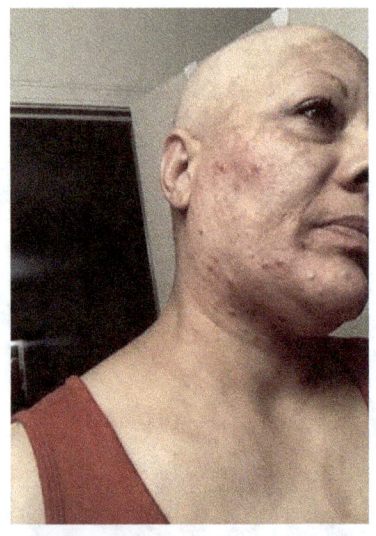

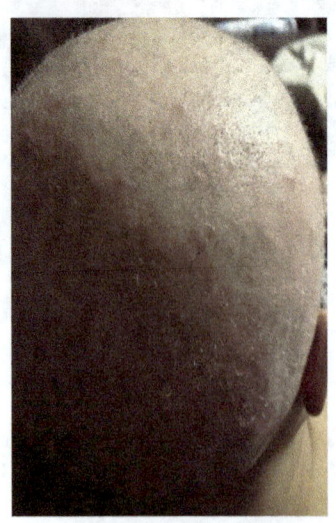

"Look Up and Live"

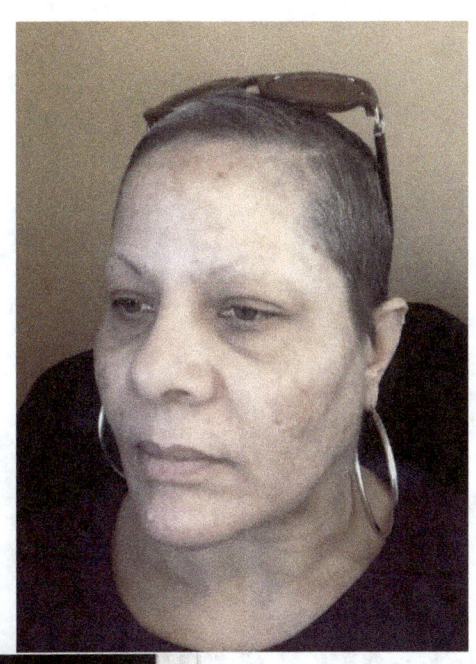

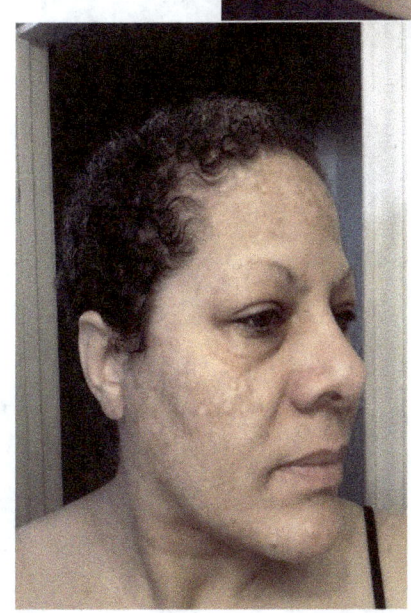

Yvette Bell

"Look Up and Live"

Yvette Bell

December 2019 - September 2020

Last Days of Survival Therapy (Chemo), Breast Surgery, Herceptin Treatment and Radiation

"Look Up and Live"

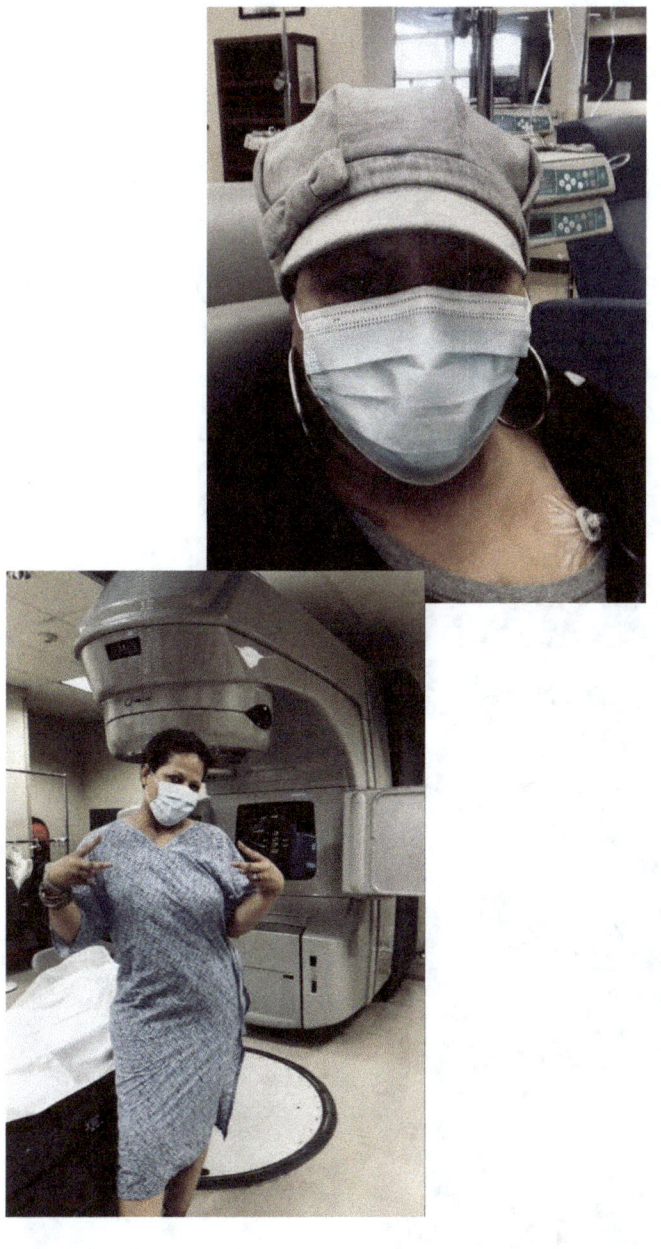

Yvette Bell

"Look Up and Live"

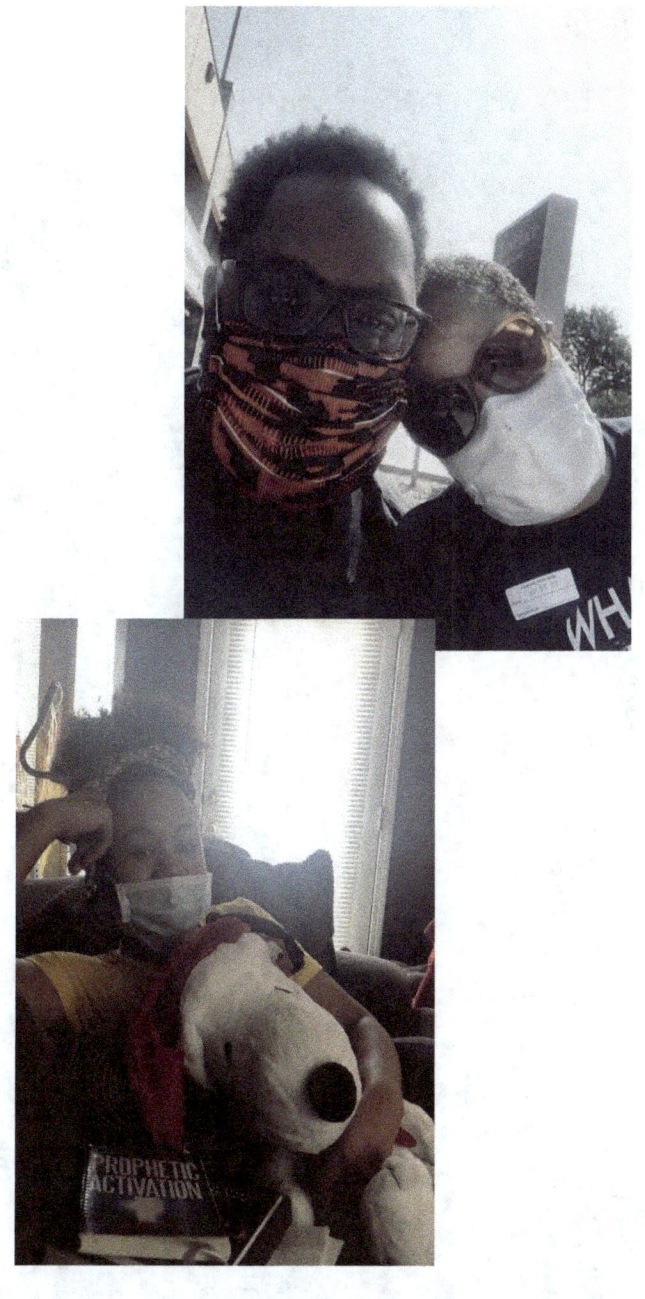

Yvette Bell

September 2020

PRAISE GOD! THERAPY OVER, CANCER FREE!

About the Author

As a licensed international evangelist, Yvette Bell serves the kingdom of God as a Spiritual Midwife and trainer, encouraging the people of God to bring forth godly assignments during the birthing seasons of life. She has ministered throughout the United States and Zambia.

Yvette's main goal is to share the message of Jesus Christ in KINGDOM AUTHORITY! Because of a deep love for the power of prayer, she coordinates a yearly community Kingdom Authority Prayer Conference, which began in 2011. Men and women of all denominations, positions, and ethnic groups come together to learn how to operate in kingdom assignment and prophetic intercession. God has manifested His healing power, sent angelic visitation, and prophetic utterance in the midst of His people as watchmen and women of God take a rightful position in kingdom principles and strategies.

In 2019 she founded "A Paradigm Shift Coaching" and became a certified John Maxwell global team member, trainer, and public speaker. Yvette wrote her first book in 2012 entitled, "A Paradigm Shift, In the Presence of the Lord."

With a passion to take the Kingdom of God to the marketplace, Yvette has over 25 years of leadership experience and has dedicated her life to serving others and working to build collaborative relationships that produce rapid, strategic outcomes.

As a result of unwavering commitment to transformational leadership, Yvette has traveled the United States and Zambia to assist individuals, non-profits, religious institutions, and governments to build capacity and create paradigm shifts in outdated systems.

As a former two-term governor appointee with the New Mexico Office of African American Affairs, ten-year State Commissioner with the New Mexico Dr. Martin Luther King Jr. Commission, thirteen-year upper management leader with the YMCA of Central New Mexico and five-year YMCA of the USA diversity and inclusion change agent, Yvette has received numerous awards and recognitions for her leadership.

Yvette has volunteered with the SteelBridge women's rescue mission, New Mexico Birthing Coalition, March of Dimes, Con Alma Health Foundation, and Albuquerque Public Schools. She is currently a board member with the New Mexico Voices for Children and employed with the Albuquerque Public School District.

Born and raised in New Mexico, Yvette is a wife, mother, and all-out lover of the Lord Jesus Christ, who believes "NO ONE" is obligated to remain in the status quo's others place them in. Everyone, when given proper support and resources, can shift to live out their full potential.

Additional Resources by the Author

Why be satisfied with the status quo when you can experience supernatural transformation? Have you ever wondered how to break past faulty thought patterns, traumatic experiences, social norms, deceptive traditions, and false religious beliefs that hold individual's captive, hindering accomplishment of God's kingdom mandate? Then this 2012 book release, "A Paradigm Shift, In the Presence of the Lord," is a great ministry resource to assist you in your quest. Because life can produce situations which manifest feelings of rejection, fear, anxiety, inferiority, and intimidation, that individuals may eventually back away from the will of God for their lives. To be fully healed and break free from such limitations, in this manuscript, you will discover:

1. How to be divinely aligned with the basic principles of God's covenant,

2. How to be healed from the toxins formed in the mind, which eventually erect fortified walls around the heart,

3. How to recognize heavenly weapons assigned to every believer that will destroy satanic hindrances,

4. How to identify change agents and midwives divinely assigned to assist with impartation and the birthing of spiritual gifts.

"This is the greatest hour of the kingdom of God. Heaven is literally opening and pouring out God's treasures upon the earth realm. For the believer, who is in divine alignment with God, the works of Christ will begin to manifest greater through the vessel, causing paradigm shifts in every facet of their lives." - Yvette Bell

This is your season to step into the fullness of your divine destiny and obtain all that God has for you. Why be satisfied with the status quo when you can experience supernatural transformation and victory during the "Paradigm Shift!"

Connect at Facebook: A Paradigm Shift Coaching & Yvette Bell Ministries

Instagram: Yvette_Bell

www.aparadigmshiftcoaching.com

"Look Up and Live"

"Today is a good day for a Paradigm Shift"!

- ➤ Frustrated, unmotivated, or distracted from current goals?

- ➤ Need help to become re-inspired and re-focused?

- ➤ Are you re-evaluating the direction of your life?

- ➤ Do you feel disconnected from your passion during a significant life change?

- ➤ Are you a leader desiring to help others accomplish goals?

- ➤ Do you long to break paradigms in your family or community?

- ➤ Ready to take the first step toward transitioning into change or gaining the courage to finish an assignment? Congratulations!

"Take the first step in faith. You don't have to see the whole staircase, just take the first step." - Dr. Martin Luther King, Jr.

"Look Up and Live"

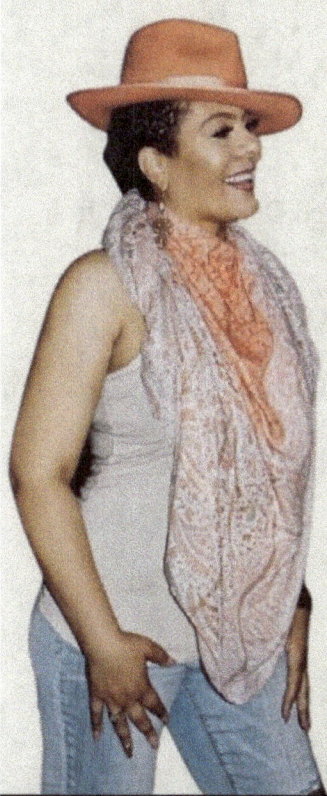

Customized services to assist with personal, professional, or business goals.

101

Endnotes

Foreword

Job 14:1, NIV

Romans 10:17, NKJV

Introduction

Psalms 139:14, NIV dominion. 2020.
In KJVBibleDictionary.com. Retrieved October 2020, from https://av1611.com/kjbp/kjv-dictionary/dominion.html

Chapter One – Taking Dominion After Diagnosis

Diagnosis. 2011. In Dictionary.com. Retrieved May 2020, from https://www.dictionary.com/browse/diagnosis

2 Timothy 3:12, KJV

John 16:33, KJV

John 9:3, KJV

2 Corinthians 4:17, NIV

Chapter Two – Voices of Influence

Micah 2:13, KJV

1 Corinthians 10:13, KJV

Genesis 50:20, KJV

Romans 8:15, KJV

Matthew 15:26, KJV

John 11:4, KJV

Hebrews 9:27, KJV

Psalms 34:19, NIV

Noisome pestilence. 2020. In Salem Media Group web-based bible commentary. Retrieved September 2020, from https://www.biblestudytools.com/commentaries/treasury-of-david/psalms-91-3.html

John 10:4, 5, NIV

John 11:4, KJV

Zephaniah 3:17, KJV

Niv Elis, Jewish Telegraphic Agency. April 26, 2017. "The 3 cancers Jews need to worry about most — and how to reduce the risks". Retrieved September 2020, from https://www.jta.org

1 Corinthians 13:9, KJV

2 Corinthians 10:5, KJV

John 8:44, KJV

Kairos Greek definition, https://en.wikidia.org/wiki/Kairos

Romans 12:2, KJV

Chapter Three – Becoming Vulnerable and Transparent

Revelations 12:11, KJV

Acts 2:42-47, KJV

Acts 3:1-11, KJV

Luke 10:25-37, KJV

I Peter 2:9-12, KJV

Ephesians 6:10-12, KJV

John 20:25-28, KJV

Romans 8:19, KJV

John 11:1-45, KJV

Galatians 2:20, KJV

Chapter Four – Transformative Trauma

Jude 1:3, KJV

2 Timothy 3:13, KJV

John 16:13, KJV

Psalms 34:19, KJV

John 10:10, KJV

Proverbs 18:21, KJV

Ecclesiastes 4:12, KJV

Philippians 4:13, KJV

I John 4:4, NLT

Ephesians 3:16

"Look Up and Live"

Chapter Five – A Family's Journey

Psalms 139:14, KJV

Mercedes Bell Journal, "Insecurities," June 12, 2020

Chapter Six – Our Story, God's Glory

Isaiah 55:8, KJV

Jeremiah 8:22, KJV

Revelations 12:11, NIV

2 Corinthians 11:23-31, NIV

Romans 8:28, KJV

Psalms 119:71, KJV

Luke 9:26, NLV

Chapter Seven – Look Up and Live

Job 14:7-9, NIV

John 3:16, KJV

Proverbs 3:12, KJV

Galatians 4:6-7, NIV

John 10:10, KJV

John 11:4, KJV

Psalms 3:3, KJV

Revelation 1:5, NKJV

www.ingramcontent.com/pod-product-compliance
Lightning Source LLC
Chambersburg PA
CBHW070938080526
44589CB00013B/1559